THE ENEMY OF GOOD

HOW TO OVERCOME PERFECTIONISM, FEAR OF FAILURE, AND INACTION SO YOU CAN FINALLY FEEL GOOD ENOUGH

JAMIE BOSWELL

CONTENTS

INTRODUCTION

No one is perfect, the saying goes, acknowledging we all have flaws. We might repeat the line with acceptance, sometimes a sigh of resignation and a shoulder shrug, sometimes with a smile and a wink. *We're only human, after all.*

In the Steinway factory in Queens, New York, Tone Regulator Bruce Campbell works on the touch and feel of the keys and the tone of a concert grand piano. He patiently measures fractions of millimeters and makes infinitesimal adjustments with various tools until he brings out the *voice* of the instrument. This is what we all want: to have a voice.

Bruce knew nothing about pianos when he started working at Steinway, and he worked his way up through Tuning, preparing the hammers for Voicing, and in Voicing for ten years. Eventually, he learned Tone Regulation from professionals with over thirty years of experience. Despite his expertise, he says, "I'm not going to look at my own piano even after I'm done and say that it's perfect because it's never perfect" (Niles, 2007).

The unique and exquisite beauty of a Steinway piano depends on the unity of mind, body, and heart; of not one but many employees, each with their specific skill - from the person selecting the wood at the sawmill to the artist playing at Carnegie Hall. They are all human and, by implication, imperfect. This is what makes beautiful, transcendental, soul-drenching music. As of yet, the perfection of machines or artificial intelligence cannot compare.

Although I am an avid music fan, I am not a musician; instead, I am a lawyer by trade. In my field, I was also trained to focus on technicalities and the "devil in the details." The training served me well for practicing law, as it can often involve meticulous and analytical work. But it also exacerbated the perfectionist tendencies already present. Early on in my career, I used to inadvertently sabotage my learning by being unwilling to make mistakes and declining challenges I did not consider myself fully equipped to overcome. Had I taken more risks, I would have made more mistakes but, as I now realize, accelerated my learning. But the idea that an error would ruin everything kept me within the confines I established for myself; I progressed slowly and surely, once I felt confident about complete understanding and control. You can imagine how frustrating it was to step so carefully, like an overly cautious toddler, as if I could not trust myself not to fall or as if falling would be the utter ruin of me. Maybe you also feel held back by the constrictions imposed by your pursuit of perfection.

When preparing a litigation brief at my first job out of law school while working at a big firm, I experienced writer's block for several days. As I inched uncomfortably close to the deadline to turn in the brief but could not start, I panicked. While searching for help online on how to get unstuck, an article advised me to put pen to paper, regardless of the content: The first draft would be bad for sure, but it didn't matter at all. What mattered most was starting the process of putting words on paper. This guidance surprisingly released me from the pressure I was placing on myself and helped me start writing. I realized my need to perform perfectly had wasted a lot of time and paralyzed me with anxiety. By seeing the first draft as a means to an end and not the end itself, it became one part of an entire process, rather than a product to be judged.

The pianist sitting down to play for a rapt audience may also seem pressured to perform perfectly, but the *perfection* of the performance relies on so much more than the artist at that moment. Let me explain. It all began far back when the piece was composed, when the piano was constructed, and when each member of the audience was born; they have their unique contexts, and the way in which they receive and interpret the music is unique to each of them. The work of the pianist is to practice well and be present to play, and when done to the best of the pianist's technical ability, it is the feeling or emotion and the sense of life that make it seem transcendental. An obsession with perfection may ensure there are no false notes, but this is not the purpose of the piece, why the artist plays, or why those listening are so moved they never forget the experience.

Although I have over 20 years of experience in the private corporate and public law sectors, I am also an avid student of psychology, fascinated by the human mind in all its complexity. I have met different people struggling within the prison of perfectionism, their creativity and their vitality stifled. I recognize the tired look in their eyes that says they are stuck chasing something they suspect is unattainable anyway, and that draws them away from what they really want. I've been where they have, within my career and personally:

overthinking, worrying, suffering from analysis paralysis, and achieving less than I was capable of. I didn't give myself a chance to try or any credit for trying. I expected a flawless finish every time.

By writing this book, I want to share my insights with others dealing with the same challenges. Our thoughts, behaviors, and beliefs manifest in every aspect of our lives and relationships; we can investigate, understand, and take ownership of them instead of letting them defeat us. As I matured, I simply could not pursue perfection anymore—at least not the impossibly high, seemingly objective, and universal standard I measured myself against. I decided to examine perfectionism as I would a legal issue: to see *what* it is, *why* it is, and whether it *works*. It turned out to be a pervasive affliction I had to overcome in all areas of my life, day by day, by practicing the techniques I will share with you in later chapters.

I have also met people who have helped me understand perfectionism from their points of view. In this book, I will tell you some of their stories, but I have changed their names for privacy.

From the outset, I want to clarify that perfectionism should not be confused with excellence and a strong work ethic. You can have incredible energy and be a high achiever, conscientious and persistent, and not be a perfectionist. This book is *not* about settling for lower standards or giving up on goals and dreams that set fire to your soul and give your life meaning. On the contrary. It *is* about overcoming the debilitating nature of perfectionism, which operates as an obstacle to attaining our goals, not as an enabler. We begin by establishing what perfectionism is, exactly, before we move deeper into how it operates in our lives and what we can do to stop it from incapacitating us.

Ultimately, this book hopes to serve as a unique, multi-disciplinary guide to provide you with insights and evidence-backed, practical tools to overcome perfectionism; it is time to fully embrace yourself for all your humanity - with compassion and true admiration for what that means.

1

THE FALLACY OF PERFECTIONISM

erfect is a lovely praise word and one many of us relish hearing about ourselves or something we have done. It conveys happiness and satisfaction, proficiency, a state of completion, and a level that cannot be improved. We often use the word subjectively, aware that when we call something perfect, we are saying how we *feel* about it; it is not a scientifically factual word devoid of opinion or emotion. It captures not only the thing but the human response to the thing - a response that feels good. In Lou Reed's song *A Perfect Day*, his idea of such a day - drinking sangria in the park, feeding animals at the zoo, and going to a movie (Reed, 1972) - is nothing like my idea of a perfect day, except his, like mine, is perfect because he spent it with someone special.

A young woman named Kim meets up with her date, Tristan. She had been working all day and did not have the time to dress up, but her eyes light up with excitement in anticipation of their evening together. She has been looking forward to it all day. Suddenly self-conscious under Tristan's appreciative smile, she smooths down her hair and asks, "Do I look okay?" She has glowing skin and shining curls, but it is more than this that draws Tristan to her; He thinks he has found "the one."

"You look perfect," Tristan replies sincerely. Perfection, like beauty, is in the eye of the beholder.

Perfection means flawlessness, the fullness of potential, and supreme and unsurpassable excellence; Perfectionism is the attitude that regards anything short of perfection as unacceptable (Merriam-Webster, 2019). Perfection is also an often-subjective noun when applied in connection to our human condition. Perfectionism, however, implies an objective standard beyond the inherently imperfect human condition. For a perfectionist, failure to attain that standard is simply unacceptable and oftentimes a source of shame. Perfectionism borrows the shine from perfection, pretending to be positive in the same way. But as we will see in the next chapter, perfectionism is most often correlated with negative and destructive mental and health outcomes, not positive ones.

Before I realized I was falling prey to perfectionism, I often came close to burning out in pursuit of excellence in my work. I was unable to reflect on what I had already achieved without feeling awkward and inadequate, always feeling I could have done better. Once or twice, colleagues rolled their eyes at me for deflecting compliments or congratulations. When I commended their work, they also seemed skeptical. One colleague said to me, "You say I did well, but I know if you had done as I did, you wouldn't be satisfied. It's as if you're saying to me, 'Well, for *you*, this is good work.'" This was someone who I respected and was becoming a close friend of mine, and what he said dismayed me. I would never treat him with condescension or expect the impossible of him. Then it struck me: My perfectionism was inadvertently making my colleagues feel judged by me. Why was I treating them, and myself, that way?

If you haven't read the children's book *Mr. Perfect*, written by Roger Hargreaves, I recommend you read it now. Mr. Perfect is a round, blue person with a neat middle parting and straight-combed hair. You can find it on internetarchive.com or YouTube, where it is read aloud by a child. It is a short video of under 5 minutes.

But if you have read it or don't mind a spoiler, I can tell you the story ends with Mr. Uppity (a very demanding and difficult character) exclaiming (1994):

> "I'm fed up with you, Mr. Perfect. And do you know why? I'll tell you. I have discovered there is a most enormous, unbearable, exasperating fault with you."
> "Would you be so kind as to tell me what that might be?" asked Mr. Perfect, as politely as ever.
> "Don't you understand?" cried Mr. Uppity. "Your fault is… that you have NO faults!" (p. 37-38)

Throughout the book, as happy as Mr. Perfect appears to be (because he is perfect after all), it is clear he is being badly treated by all and should stand up for himself, even if it means he is less than perfect. Over time, I realized that standing up for myself meant accepting myself as less than perfect and insisting I be treated fairly by others and, especially, by myself.

We've all heard the idiom: *If it's worth doing, it's worth doing well*. But there is also the counterargument: *If it's worth doing, it's worth doing badly*. Not everything we do needs to be done well, especially small, everyday things we depend on. Do I really need to wake up completely refreshed after a night of unbroken, quality sleep; have a complete and nutritious breakfast worthy of an

Instagram post; squeeze in my hour workout and meditation session before showering for work; dress in trendy clothes that define my unique style before heading to work on time, with an upbeat attitude, ready to be productive—every day? It's worth it to sleep, to wake up, to eat breakfast and be healthy, to be hygienic, to be aware of one's appearance, to work, to stay optimistic—so worth it, in fact, it's worthwhile doing badly but consistently. The *doing* is more important than how well or badly it is done.

Besides, doing something *well* does not mean doing it *excellently*. And one person's *excellence* is another's *average*. There will always be someone else who does a thing better than you. Except for being you: Only you can do that.

Perfectionists can be both high and low achievers; low achievement can be the direct result of perfectionism, causing the sufferer low self-esteem, depression, and the inability to take concrete action or trust their instincts, among other negative effects. A perfectionist might not agree with the quote, "Done is better than perfect" (Sandberg, 2013) or that other saying that inspired the title of this book, "Perfect is the enemy of good." And yet, I hope after reading this book, you will understand and embrace the wisdom behind these aphorisms.

PERFECTIONISM AND ITS DIMENSIONS

According to Prof. Joachim Stoeber and Prof. Julian H. Childs (2011):

> Perfectionism is a personality disposition characterized by striving for flawlessness and setting excessively high standards for performance accompanied by tendencies for overly critical evaluations. It is a disposition that pervades all areas of life, particularly work and school, and may also affect one's personal appearance and social relationships. (p. 2)

Stoeber and Childs found *perfectionistic striving* (striving toward being as good as one can be) had a better effect on well-being and adjustment than belief in *perfectionist concerns,* when acceptance or esteem is granted by others according to conditions being met. In this light, perfectionism could be seen as normal, or *adaptive,* or neurotic, or *maladaptive*: the former, when a person has high perfectionistic strivings but low perfectionist concerns, and the latter, when a person has higher perfectionistic concerns than perfectionistic strivings.

Extensive research by Dr. Paul Hewitt and Dr. Gordon Flett over the last twenty-odd years reveals that trait perfectionism is multi-faceted within the following three main, differentiated, but often interrelated, dimensions:

Self-Oriented Perfectionism (SOP)

This is the only dimension that can, potentially, carry positive outcomes associated with personal high-achievement strivings.

Self-oriented perfectionism may be associated with desirable characteristics such as conscientiousness, adaptive coping or resilience, positive emotion, and mental well-being and adjustment. One is motivated to participate and perform well, and self-esteem rises with one's accomplishments. Simply being motivated or inspired raises one's self-perception and problems and setbacks are regarded as opportunities that can lead to progress.

But unrealistic expectations and self-recrimination can also lead to a negative self-image and perpetual dissatisfaction with oneself. SOP has been equally correlated with depression, as setting unrealistic standards results in more frequent failure, and severe self-evaluation heightens the significance of the failure; it is also related to somatoform symptoms (physical symptoms in response to psychological stress), hypomania (a less severe form of mania), and alcoholism (Hellman, 2016).

Those with maladaptive SOP tend to:

- set exacting standards for themselves.
- exhaust themselves trying to perform optimally.
- try to do the best they can at everything they do.
- want to be *the best* out of everyone at what they do.
- think that doing/being the best should come naturally.
- routinely criticize themselves.
- worry about making mistakes.
- procrastinate.
- suffer from *analysis paralysis*.
- agonize over decisions.

Socially Prescribed Perfectionism (SPP)

This dimension involves facets relating to *perfectionistic concerns* about mistakes, second-guessing oneself and doubting one's decisions, worrying about what others think, and a sense of discrepancy between expectations and results.

Negative outcomes include mental health issues and overall dissatisfaction in life. Perfection seems to be imposed on them from the outside world, and criticism is perceived as coming from others, detrimentally impacting one's self-esteem.

If Kim's wish to look good is based solely on what Tristan thinks of her appearance, she may be reacting to socially prescribed perfectionism. Although Tristan says she looks perfect, Kim will not accept this as honesty, or Tristan's truth, because she will believe there is an objective standard of perfection to which everyone ascribes. Even when she has the time to spend getting ready for a date, she may not be completely satisfied with the way she looks. She may also feel Tristan's answer about her looking perfect just confirms this is exactly what her date expects of her, adding more stress and demands on her appearance.

Socially prescribed perfectionists tend to:

- try to live up to standards set by others.
- feel put upon by others, especially by those close to them.
- compare themselves to others.
- fear others are more successful than them.
- feel threatened by others' success.
- feel like *square pegs in round holes* or as if they don't *belong*.
- enjoy impressing others with their success.

Other-Oriented Perfectionism (OOP)

In contrast to the two dimensions discussed above, this dimension of perfectionism directs criticism not at oneself, but at others. Perfection in others is considered the most important. The other-oriented perfectionist aims to be socially dominant instead of nurturing, cooperative or empathetic, and often, has unreasonable standards for their family members, significant other, co-workers, and friends.

If Kim were to expect Tristan to admire her no matter what she looked like or did and expect him to always look and act "perfect" himself, she would be exhibiting OOP. Those on the receiving end of this type of perfectionism often perceive having to consistently measure up to someone else's expectation of perfection as unfair and draining, especially if the perfectionist is supposed to love or care about them.

Other-oriented perfectionists tend to:

- feel annoyed by those who are not trying to improve.
- expect others to fulfill all the potential they may possess.
- be extra demanding to work with/for.
- become agitated when people who are close to them make mistakes.

- make people feel worse rather than good about themselves and feel compelled to routinely point out their mistakes and faults.

These three components of perfectionism and their characteristics constitute a clinical model (a complete and verifiable explanation of clinical use in understanding perfectionism) known as the Comprehensive Model of Perfectionist Behavior (Hewitt, 2020). This model has been helpful in the treatment of perfectionism as a maladaptive behavior.

If we were to compare the dimensions mentioned above to scriptwriting: SOP is like writing a script for yourself to follow. SPP is like following a script someone else has written for you. And OOP is like writing a script for everyone else to follow. Nonperfectionism is like reading the script, adopting whatever is suitable and meaningful, and abandoning it in favor of informed improvisation. Anyone who has watched the funny American TV series Whose Line Is It Anyway? might agree improv can often result in more creative and delightful content than strict adherence to a script.

CAN PERFECTIONISM EVER BE BENEFICIAL?

As mentioned earlier, the desire to excel should not be confused with the desire to be perfect.

While all three dimensions of perfectionism discussed above are responsible for destructive perfectionism, the first (Self-Oriented Perfectionism) may have a beneficial aspect related to the desire to excel. Kim, meeting up with Tristan for their date and wanting to look good, displays what could be seen as a positive trait of self-oriented perfectionism by having her own idea of what looking good is. She wants to look her best for important dates that matter to her and is pleased when she does and disappointed when she doesn't. Still, Kim understands the date can go ahead as planned, regardless. Her sense of self-worth and enjoyment doesn't depend on how she looks. She will be more willing to believe Tristan's statement about her because she will better understand the subjective nature of the word *perfect*.

When I went for job interviews after law school, I answered questions about my weaknesses as I had been advised to do back then - by saying, "I am a perfectionist." Perfectionism was widely regarded as a so-called weakness that could be a strength in the workplace, promising meticulous attention to detail, excellent organizational skills, and strict self-discipline.

Working in the latter half of the 20th century, Professor of Counseling and Educational Psychology Don Hamachek believed normal or adaptive perfectionists set realistic standards for themselves and could adjust or lower standards as situations required, finding pleasure in striving to attain these standards. Neurotic or maladaptive perfectionists, on the other hand, demanded unrealistic, inflexibly high, if not unattainable, standards and found their efforts unsatisfactory (Hamachek, 1978).

More recently, Dr. Paul Hewitt has argued no form of perfectionism can ever be beneficial. Perfectionism is a risk factor for depression and suicide, he notes, and perfectionists "are generally individuals who live pretty unhappily and have dissatisfied lives. They seemingly have learned the route to social connection is to fit in with the world, and to have self-worth is by being perfect or by appearing to others as perfect" (University of British Columbia, 2016).

He illustrates this with a story of one of his patients who achieved an A+ for a course but lamented that if he had been better, he would not have had to work so hard to achieve the grade. According to Dr. Hewitt, therapy that asks perfectionists to lower their standards is less effective than therapy that focuses on "the need to be accepted and cared for" (Benson, 2003). Perfectionism results from needing to be accepted and cared for, and returning to the root of what triggered perfectionism leads to more effective treatment.

3 MYTHS ABOUT PERFECTIONISM

Professor of Psychology Thomas Curran believes that perfectionism can be measured on a spectrum in everyone, and it comes from a place of deficit and discontent. He also thinks perfectionism is encouraged by massive advertising and consumerism. Professor Curran describes the following shared beliefs about perfectionism as myths (Lisbon, 2022):

Myth #1: Perfectionism means high standards

As you know by now, high standards are distinct from perfectionism. High standards challenge and inspire, while perfectionism demands and intimidates, like a bully who is only satisfied by putting down his victim. Ambitious standards are about ability, while perfectionism is about inability to achieve the impossible.

Myth #2: Perfectionists are more likely to succeed

Because perfectionists tend to be more afraid of failure than non-perfectionists, they take fewer risks and avoid situations that might show them at a disadvantage. This can make them less likely to succeed in the long term; success requires a certain boldness, courage, and not being afraid of sometimes looking like a fool. For genuine risk-takers who want to fail fast and grow faster, it doesn't matter if they do something dumb or embarrassing. Their primary objective is not to make a good impression but to gain knowledge and expand their horizons.

Myth #3: Perfection is attainable

As we've already seen, there is no objective definition of perfection within the confines of human experience. It differs slightly from person to person and is far more subjective than we believe. What is certain is it is always just out of reach. Because perfection is a moving target, reliant on personal experience and tendencies, culture, and beliefs, among other things, no one can epitomize it for long. Maybe the most one can hope for is fifteen minutes of so-called perfection.

British Secret Service Intelligence Officer Frank Foley rescued over 10,090 Jews from Nazi execution. He was short in stature, "small and a little pot-bellied," wore round glasses, and flew under the radar while being an effective intelligence agent (Sedgewick, 2019). This unassuming presence may have been to his advantage and to the men, women, and children he rescued. Foley was not perfect, but he found himself in the right place at the right time to do the only right thing. One might say that without the terrible faults of others, Foley would not have been so extraordinary. In this way, his perfection in those actions relied on the imperfection of others. But his compassion and courage make him a hero today. Benno Cohen, a witness in Adolf Eichmann's trial in 1961, described Foley as "one of the greatest among the nations of the world" (Yad Vashem, 2023).

Other historical figures were similarly underestimated on the surface but became transcendental, not for their perfection, but for their actions or the legacy they created. Vincent Van Gogh, whose story is also well-known, received little positive feedback for his work during his lifetime. Today, he is widely regarded as an outstanding and still influential artist.

Sometimes, a sense of someone's perfection is brought about by factors beyond any person's control, including the control of those later exalted to such elevated standards. Artist Alma Thomas started her art career only after retiring from teaching at seventy. She is now considered one of America's greatest 20th-century artists and role models. This success could not have been planned or considered attainable by most people at the time, including Alma.

Cultural exaltation is primarily out of our hands; perfectionism would like to make you think otherwise.

PERFECTIONISM ON THE RISE

In the United States and Europe, perfectionism is rising due to competitive individualism and increasing materialism among the young (Curran & Hill, 2019). Individualism involves distinguishing the individual from the collective. It emphasizes the agency of every person to fulfill their destiny. Live your best life! is a common refrain or, Be the best you, you can be!

At the same time, people may worry about letting down those around them who are part of their group or inner circle. And the world seems to be in permanent crisis (summed up in the portmanteau permacrisis), moving unceasingly from one political or natural disaster to another and overwhelmed by climatic change. People are not only expected to prosper individually but make the world a better place, often needing help to make sense of mutually exclusive ambitions.

Under stress, humans have an automatic biochemical response that initiates a fight, flight, freeze, or fawn response. Even when a threat is not physical, our bodies are programmed to react as our ancestors would have long ago in an ongoing fight for survival. If they could not stand and fight or flee, they would have stayed still or fawned like a dog rolling onto its back in submission to say, "Don't destroy me!" We still instinctively behave along these lines without deciding to do so; stress reduces our decision-making ability as blood moves away from the brain and into the limbs for physical performance.

Performance anxiety occurs when a person fears performing and falling short or failing. They are usually afraid to make a fool of themselves. It can happen when a person must perform on stage or when delivering a speech, more commonly known as stage fright. It can also be a perpetual state of mind in which a person feels like life is a performance. They might have a mild sense of discomfort, a strong reluctance to participate, or reach a state of such severe anxiety they have a panic attack. At their onset, the symptoms accompanying a panic attack may convince people they are having a heart attack, frightening them even more. They may experience trembling, shortness of breath, heart palpitations, and a sense of detachment from their bodies, over which they have lost control; they may even lose vision, feeling in their extremities, and consciousness.

In Scandinavia, perfectionism is receiving increasing attention due to rising concern about the mental health of adolescents struggling with demands to succeed and excel. Prof. Ole Jacob Masden, in his book *Deconstructing Scandinavia's Achievement Generation* (2021), notes how neoliberalism or free-market capitalism prioritizes the market without offering sufficient psychosocial support beyond the goods, brands, services, and experiences of consumer culture; when youth fail to live up to idealized norms in a society that says everything is possible, they may feel ashamed and depressed. Adolescents, particularly girls, growing up in resourceful schools and areas are especially inclined to internalize the notion of an achievement-driven society where one's social identity depends on the ability to perform in different areas such as school, sports, social media, and so on (Krogh & Madden, 2023).

Generation Z is colloquially called the generation of performance anxiety. Generation Z (or Gen Z) are those born between 1997 and 2012, who will be between 11 and 26 at the time of writing this book. The upper-middle class Gen Z grew up in a world online, with most of them able to access technology any time of the day. Online access means they have instant access to more global knowledge, news, and opinions than the generations before them. More research resources are available to them, and they can access more information, advertising, conjecture, and misinformation. They are more aware of the ethical implications of what they say and do and have pressure to be politically, socially, and environmentally responsible. They keep up with the latest posts, ideas, and trends from celebrities and influencers on social media. They can compare products, reviews, and demand better service and quality of products. Expressing their identity and individuality is important, and they are more inclined to search for meaningful experiences that enrich their lives. While one may expect the endless range and possibilities of the internet to result in a more profound sense of curiosity and capability, it imparts a greater level of anxiety.

The next chapter will cover anxiety brought about by social media—a subject for a whole book in itself—in more detail. Youth tend to turn to social media (especially video platforms) for help with anxiety, and it is affordable and easy to access by technologically minded people (Garnham, 2022). They may feel protected by anonymity or less vulnerable than speaking to people they know in person. But they are also more likely to access misinformation or advice from unqualified people or strangers with hidden agendas. Excessive screen time can aggravate anxiety and depression.

Social media also encourages self-promotion, including pretense and comparison. Perceived successes include everything from living in scenic surroundings to going on exciting holidays, achieving academically or in sports, overcoming the odds, rescuing those in need, having romantic relationships, raising happy children, cooking, or eating well, and so the list goes on. Another case of Mr. Perfect, whose life is perfect, and even when it is not, it doesn't matter because he is perfect. Or is he?

Wanting to appear perfect to others is another dimension of perfectionism. Let's take a closer look at why one might cling to a semblance of perfection, like a hermit crab clinging to the empty shell of another species.

2

KEEPING UP WITH THE JONESES

I t is human nature to reflect on one's identity: who one is, and who one wants to be. We reflect more on our identity at different periods in our lives, most often during adolescence and then again during our second adolescence, or what is more commonly known as a *midlife crisis*.

Although there's bound to be a gap at specific periods between who one is and who one wants to be, someone self-accepting will base their aspirations on the solid foundation of what they know and accept of themselves. They will advance with a sense of inner calm, as they reach subjectively important, achievable milestones they set for themselves. A cousin of mine described her self-assurance as a solid stone within her that would never change or disappear; no matter what happens, it remains constant and gives her strength and stability.

Professor Emeritus of Psychology William E. Herman writes:

> Identity formation is about the complex way humans establish a unique view of self and is characterized by continuity and inner unity. It is, therefore, highly related to terms such as the self, self-concept, values, and personality development. The goal of personal identity formation is to establish a coherent view of self through the process of normal human development. Abnormal development could be viewed as the establishment of an incoherent self-characterized by a discontinuity or the lack of inner unity. Although the benchmarks of identity formation are most easily observed at the adolescent and adult levels of development, a fledgling identity a person develops during his/her childhood experiences. At the core of identity formation is the human personality. (p. 779–781)

As social creatures, humans do not develop individual identities in isolation; they are linked to relationships.

Our distinct roles within our lives are incorporated into whom we consider ourselves to be, and they can change throughout our lives: I may strongly identify as a daughter when I am young, but as my life progresses, I may identify as independent of my parents. I have several co-existing identities: friend, lawyer, lover, wife, mother, leader, etc. Nevertheless, there is a core sense of self or an authentic self that lies beneath my roles; it tells me I am valuable because I *am*, not because I *do*. Satisfaction and a sense of being true to oneself come when I do things that express who I am. They are the things for which I have a natural, innate capability, and they have meaning and purpose for me.

However, as society often places more value in what we do (or do not) than what we *are*, we have learned that we receive appreciation and validation when we complete tasks well or accomplish goals deemed worthy or valuable. Even when we do what we love and are skilled for, the experience can be ruined by a sense that we are not accomplishing something "worthwhile" according to those external societal standards.

Perfectionism draws us toward achievement that does not necessarily have anything to do with our authentic selves. It fools us into thinking that what we do and how we do it is more important than why we do it as a part of who we are. An increase in self-esteem rewards us as we gain the admiration of others. On the other hand, self-esteem obtained this way can vanish at any time due to imperfection and the loss of others' esteem. Perfectionists find themselves in a predicament where they must remain perfect or lose the respect of others and face rejection.

Those struggling with perfectionism often feel the need to *appear* perfect to project overall perfection. To appear perfect, one must display or exhibit perfection as it is conceived by oneself and others; similarly, imperfection must be disguised or hidden. This dimension of perfectionism heavily relies on measuring or evaluation one person's perfection against another's. Thus, it results in comparison, which, as the saying goes, is the thief of joy.

To "keep up with The Joneses" means to show one is as good as other people by getting what they have and doing what they do (Merriam-Webster, 2022). In the past, those *other people* were usually in one's neighborhood or community, but today we have neighbors throughout the world whom we can observe from proximity online. We might even know more about people in other countries than we do about those living next door. People next door may hold little interest for us as we follow the lives of those who seem much more glamorous, intelligent, or perfect. Keeping up with The Joneses has become much harder.

Moreover, keeping up with them has less appeal than outdoing them!

One sure way to show we are keeping up with The Joneses is with material possessions, but these possessions symbolize much more than what they are. Suppose The Joneses have a state-of-the-art, new, and modern kitchen - it suggests they have refined taste they can afford, they value themselves and their mealtimes, and they make great hosts for parties and get-togethers at home. To keep up with the *foodie* Joneses, all I need is to upgrade my kitchen. Or do I?

My ambition to be a skilled lawyer emerged in high school after winning an award in the debate club. This accolade gave me a temporary sense of accomplishment. It made me optimistic about my prospects for a career in law. However, during my four-year bachelor's degree in college, I was disappointed I only graduated *cum laude* (not *magna*). I disappointed myself yet again when I didn't graduate in the top 10% of my class when completing my Juris Doctor degree over the next three years; In retrospect, my grades should have been more than good enough.

From then on, I tried to keep up with others in my profession, not only at the firm at which I worked but in successful law firms around the world. I wanted to stand out and soar. All this while improving the judicial system and making a significant difference in people's lives. I also started to equate material possessions with signs of success. If I wore a tailored designer pant suit, I would appear to be focused on my career with a certain masculine functionality combined with feminine charm. Upgrading to the newest version of a smartphone meant I was reachable, up-to-date, and organized. Driving an expensive car meant I was *going places*. Wearing trendy gym clothes meant I was serious about my health and fitness.

I also felt intimidated by well-respected people in my industry, but with time and more maturity, I realized it was only by keeping their company that I would learn from them. In earlier years, I found it difficult to let them see my imperfections or ask what they might consider "stupid" questions. It took me years to finally learn I was not supposed to know everything, that asking questions was an investment in myself worth making, regardless of what others thought, and that showing imperfections, and not going out of my way to hide every one of them at all costs, gave me the power of *vulnerability*. When you are transparent about what you do not know, what you need from someone, or what your doubts and weaknesses are, it will often result in a powerful bond with those with whom you've decided to share your vulnerability. You will find that, in turn, they are more willing to reciprocate in kind.

INTERPERSONAL PERFECTIONISM

Human beings are social animals, and our interaction with one another means a lot to us.

Self-Presentation

Self-presentation is the way we present ourselves during interactions with others. Across the three dimensions of perfectionism discussed in the previous chapter, it may reveal itself in different ways. Self-oriented perfectionists may want to present themselves in a way that makes them feel good about themselves because they believe they deserve it. Socially prescribed perfectionists may be more inclined to focus on influencing others to think well of them, regardless of their beliefs. Other-oriented perfectionists' self-presentation will be one of non-disclosure and distance, where the focus is redirected from themselves to others.

Perfectionist self-presentation is related to self-esteem. Perfectionist representation of the self is a desire to present oneself favorably to others in a maladaptive way. By turning only your *good side* to others, you come across as only a fraction of a person, a flat silhouette instead of a three-dimensional one.

Perfectionist self-presentation involves the interpersonal expression of perfectionism, composed of the following three sub-dimensions (Hewitt et al., 2003):

1. Perfectionist self-promotion

Perfectionist self-promotion involves promoting oneself as perfect by displaying one's perfection for others to see.

Social media fuels this dimension, enabling us to post self-glorifying images and texts. A narcissist pursuing an idyllic self-image might take this as far as possible. But even a mentally healthy person might "pridefully promote an image of perfect capability and invulnerability in pursuit of others' admiration" (Sherry et al. 2007). There is presently little regulation of social media, and almost anything goes.

An example of self-promotion from my life would be how, as a young lawyer without much experience, I chose to discuss only my successful cases. Perfectionist self-promotion usually extends to every area of life.

However, I was so wrapped up in my work, I knew I couldn't pretend to be perfect in every other sphere too. I spent insufficient quality time with friends and family, and felt I did not have enough time to devote to things I enjoyed, such as reading, creative writing, cooking, etc. Besides, if I couldn't do these things properly, I didn't want to do them at all. My work had to be perfect to compensate for my blatant neglect of other areas.

2. Non-display of imperfection

Non-display of imperfection entails avoiding the display of one's imperfection in one's behavior.

As a young lawyer, I remember wanting to brush over my unsuccessful cases with colleagues when chatting at networking events. I thought mentioning a single failure, however relevant to the conversation at hand, would taint all my successes, in the same way a rotten apple causes all the apples around it to rot. Moreover, I would concentrate on my litigation skills and skirt discussions about other parts of my life or work because they seemed too faulty and lacking. I would stick to the subject for which I had the "best record" because it cast me in the best light. Other subjects highlighted my ignorance or lack of expertise. Non-display preserves an image of invincibility; as mentioned previously, it also keeps you from experiencing the power of vulnerability in relationships.

3. Non-disclosure of imperfection

Non-disclosure of imperfection means hiding one's imperfection or mistakes.

If one makes any errors, one tries to correct them or make up for them without telling anyone, hoping no one has noticed.

We all know that person at work who, no matter how obvious to their colleagues they dropped the ball on a project, will never admit they are at fault, and will offer up excuses for why the project was delayed (except for their actions or lack thereof). And if this person becomes aware of the mistake prior to everyone else, they will go out of their way to hide it. Not everyone who behaves this way is a perfectionist; however, this behavior does present a classic example of this type of self-presentation.

Perfectionist self-promoters also exhibit elevated levels of self-monitoring behaviors; in response to external situations and environments, they adapt how they present themselves. They take their cues from other people or the contexts in which they find themselves, either to obtain the approval or attention of others or to safeguard themselves from disapproval or rejection. They may say things to impress or amuse the people around them. They can anticipate what would please others and are willing to change their opinions to conform to the group; they are good at reflecting on what they see around them or may ask for advice about how to behave or what to do. They take control from someone else's perspective, hyper-aware of how others perceive them.

People with low self-monitoring behaviors tend to behave more according to internal impetus. As social animals, self-monitoring is expected and effective in helping us get along. Nevertheless, self-monitoring to present oneself as perfect can result from a lost or insubstantial identity. If identity depends on self-esteem, it cannot remain stable; it will rise and fall according to how we perceive ourselves and how we believe others perceive us.

Trait perfectionism and perfectionistic self-presentation overlap, but while "trait perfectionism focuses on motives and dispositions related to attaining perfection, perfectionistic self-presentation focuses on expressing one's perfection to others. In other words, trait perfectionism represents what perfectionism *is*, and perfectionistic self-presentation represents what perfectionism *does*" (Sherry et al., 2007).

In her 2016 honor scholar thesis, Emily Hellman of DePauw University discusses how early psychological research focused on perfectionism as a personality trait or the manifestation of internal characteristics. She indicates trait perfectionism could be beneficial if it motivated people to attain their full potential and be exemplary human beings. But if it results in imposing unrealistic expectations on oneself or others, it is psychologically maladaptive. At the turn of the 21st century, she reveals, research uncovered perfectionism is often accompanied not only by a desire to *be* perfect but, as we have seen earlier, to *appear* perfect.

Hellman observes the main three dimensions of trait perfectionism (self-oriented perfectionism, socially prescribed perfectionism, and other-oriented perfectionism, as discussed in the previous chapter) are related to the three dimensions of self-presentation (perfectionist self-promotion, non-display of imperfection, and non-disclosure of imperfection discussed above). She believes self-oriented perfectionism and socially prescribed perfectionism are strongly associated with perfectionist self-promotion and non-display of imperfection, while socially prescribed perfectionism correlates with non-disclosure of imperfection, which indicates an unwillingness to disclose personal mistakes to avoid being judged by others. "The three facets of perfectionist self-representation produce a variety of interpersonal problems which in turn result in social disconnection, alienation and a sense of not belonging" (Hellman, 2016).

Thus, the desire to appear perfect can impair mental well-being and lead to suffering and self-destructive behavior.

3

THE ROOTS OF PERFECTIONISM

What sparks perfectionism into flame? It starts as a flickering tongue that quickly rages, consuming time and energy, eating away at life until there is no more fuel; then, the flame sputters, and there is burnout. If you have experienced or are experiencing this wildfire of perfectionism, as I once did, I want to assure you - you are not alone: I have been there, surrounded by the blazing wall that seemed to close in on me and left me consistently exhausted. It may sound melodramatic, but those in a similar predicament may comprehend how menacing and single-minded perfectionism can be. It can make you sick, aiming to turn you into a shadow of yourself and eventually even kill you.

I also want to assure you there is a way out and you can put out this fire yourself and with the help of others. Chapters 6 through 8 discuss practical and effective techniques to do this, but before we get there, let us look at a question I asked myself often and that you are probably asking too. How did I get here?

Perfectionists want to assume complete control over themselves and may easily blame themselves for their difficult—sometimes unbearable—situation. They are less likely to admit they are in trouble, especially trouble that is of their own making. An admission would mean they have taken a wrong turn and must *go back,* after investing so much in getting where they are.

It took me longer than you may think to progress from my breakthrough in preparing that first litigation brief after law school to the state of perpetual imperfection I can now gracefully accept. There were ups and downs, suppressions, and regressions, before a lasting change.

I clearly recall one day early in my career, sitting in a dark building with only the light of a desk lamp shining on my papers, working late into the night. As evening drew near, the sound of another lawyer typing away or rifling through their files sounded like an alarm bell to me; The competition to succeed and make partner as early as possible was a large shadow, looming over most of my days. As unbalanced as my life was at the time, I made sure I always "looked" the part: a legal powerhouse, smartly attired, immaculately groomed, composed, and alert. I ate healthily and rose early every morning to exercise.

But one morning, I could not get up. Instead of a three-mile run, I wanted to take a three-day nap. The prospect of continuing as I had been—ready and prepared, burning the midnight oil to make sure my cases were well-written, watertight, and covered every eventuality—left me drained. I wondered if I would ever move again. After speaking to my sister about how I felt, I took her advice and asked for a leave of absence for a week. My sister came over to my apartment to watch over me, which although was very welcome and appreciated, also embarrassed me, since I was a grown woman and should not have needed her help at all (I thought at the time). I blamed myself mostly, or the part of myself that had taken charge of me and bullied me. I felt divided against myself. I knew better than to berate myself, either for expecting too much or failing to deliver.

I also understood choice and change were possible. I had come to a crossroads. I wanted to understand how I had gotten there and what causes perfectionism in the first place.

6 PREVALENT CAUSES

Genetics

Going back as far as I could, I considered the fundamental biological building blocks that formed me. In my quest to figure out if I had been born this way, I remembered what a dog trainer and behaviorist I had met a while back told me: people were unreasonable to expect certain behaviors from certain breeds: Thoroughbred dogs had characteristics firmly entrenched in them, and to turn a sled dog into a guard dog or a herder into a lapdog was simply impossible. Did I inherit my perfectionist trait from my mother, who was undoubtedly a perfectionist too? I wondered. If so, what hope was there of changing? Wouldn't I return to built-in, conditioned behavior?

"It's part of my personality to be a perfectionist," I thought. But how much of my perfectionistic personality was genetic, and how much was due to my upbringing and environment?

Trait theory of personality has identified five main, universal traits that can co-exist and show up to higher or lesser degrees in one person. Here are the five personality traits and their estimated heritability, according to studies of identical and fraternal twins (Cherry, 2022):

1. Openness

~61% Heritable.

Also known as openness to experience, this trait involves imaginativeness, creativity, curiosity, and a wide range of interests. A high-scoring open personality will enjoy abstract thinking and tackling new challenges. A person who scores low on openness will be more resistant to change, unimaginative, conventional, and dislike working out theoretical concepts.

2. Conscientiousness

~44% Heritable.

Conscientious people are thoughtful, organized, goal-oriented, and analytical, with strong impulse control. Someone scoring low in this area may procrastinate or fail to meet deadlines.

3. Extraversion

~53% Heritable.

Extraversion indicates sociability, communicativeness, and expressiveness. Extraverts usually feel energized after being with other people. Those who score low in this trait tend to prefer solitude to company and feel drained after being with other people. Unlike those scoring high in extraversion, they are not talkative and like to think of what to say before they speak.

4. Agreeableness

~41% Heritable.

Altruistic, cooperative, and considerate people are agreeable types. Those who score low in this area are more inclined to be careless of others, insulting, competitive, and manipulative.

5. Neuroticism

~41% Heritable.

Neurotics have sad, moody, anxious, and emotionally unstable tendencies. A low score here will be emotionally resilient and happier.

A study testing a sample of 678 Romanian twins resulted in univariate estimates that showed perfectionistic concerns and neuroticism are 32–46% or moderately heritable (Burcaș & Crețu, 2021). As the percentages reveal, there is enough leeway for us to work with if we wish to influence our personalities toward outlooks that make us happier. It is good news genes play only a moderate part in forming our personality.

I score high in four out of the five personality traits, but I'm not entirely sure if I inherited or acquired them. I love to travel off the beaten path and hang out with the locals in new places. I enjoy staying fit and the strength and agility I get from it. Awareness of being in my own body helps to center, calm, and empower me. I love reading and, when I cannot read, I listen to podcasts, especially true-crime ones that bring out the "Sherlock Holmes" in me. I am invested in humanity and enjoy the company and conversation of a diverse range of people. My deepest sense of satisfaction comes from helping others understand themselves; there is nothing better than helping someone realize their thoughts, behaviors, and beliefs manifest in every aspect of their lives and relationships, and they can alter the course of their lives by taking ownership of these.

Although I scored low on neuroticism, perfectionism took me to a place where self-chastising thoughts over-whelmed me. I was no longer interested in the things or people I used to enjoy, withdrawn and exhausted. I discovered the perfectionism I secretly prized had pervaded so many areas of my life and ultimately debilitated me. Finally, I had to address it for what it was and set out on a healing journey that began with understanding how I became a perfectionist. It might have been genetic, but only to a degree.

High Parental Expectations

Many psychological problems stem back to childhood experiences, especially parent-child relationships. Our parents or primary caregivers are the first people with whom we form meaningful bonds and the first people to model adult human identity for us. There is no such thing as a *perfect* parent.

Every parent has their philosophy on how to rear their children, but one of the main functions of a parent is to demonstrate unconditional love towards their child. On the other hand, I think a parent must establish boundaries to give a child a sense of security and structure and take some of the burden of decision-making from their shoulders. The parent-child relationship must change when the child grows into adulthood;

although adulthood may come early or late, it comes when the child assumes agency and no longer relies on their parents' direction. I have met many adults who think they are their own people and yet resent their parents—or rather an idea about their parents—for still influencing their present tense from the remote past. Our parents will always be a part of us because we internalize them so readily when we are young.

Many people complain about having parents who were never pleased by their efforts but continually urged them to try harder next time. I've heard parents say they treat their children harshly and demand a lot from them because this is how the *real* world will treat them as adults. Sometimes, parents whose children do not perform well will accuse them of being lazy or having a poor attitude - not understanding perfectionism also leads to procrastination and reluctance to perform. Perfectionism may be easier to live with when things are going well. But when tasks are complex, perfectionists may turn away from them, feeling overwhelmed. If young people feel their parents' love and approval depend on their performance, they will not feel *good enough* unless they keep aiming for higher goals.

There are also those well-intentioned parents who worry about their children and doubt they will manage without parental support one day. These parents may put pressure on their children for their good, they believe, exhorting them to do well in their studies so they will enter dependable and well-paid jobs.

From a parent's perspective, they see the world is changing at warp speed and worry that if their children do not excel early on in an ever-increasing competitive work environment, they will fall behind and never find their feet.

However, parental grand expectations are not always concerned with their children's financial futures. Parents may also expect a great deal from their children when it comes to carrying on the family's cultural values.

Xiu's parents had high-performance expectations of him. They had limited studies and were from a generation that experienced high political and economic uncertainty in China. After immigrating to Canada, they sacrificed their time, energy, and earnings to ensure Xiu, the first generation born there, had the opportunities they never did. In return, they expected him to achieve high grades, play the clarinet professionally, excel in sports, and always be on his best behavior, especially when it came to showing deference to his elders. Xiu, aware of all his parents poured into his education and development, often felt torn between them and his peers, whose parents seemed so easy going and indulgent by comparison. "They say every-thing they've done is for me," he confided in his best friend one day, "but it feels like it's all for them - like they want me to live for them."

He graduated top of his class and was offered a scholar-ship to further his clarinet and music studies, which he accepted at his parents' insistence. "You ought to be grateful," his father rebuked him when he seemed unsure, "Not everyone gets offered a chance like this!"

Xiu also felt obliged to continue ice hockey at a competitive level but soon sustained an acute injury that put a hold on both sports and music studies. When he returned to music school, he found he had fallen far behind and even struggled to play as he used to. Destructive perfectionist tendencies that had already developed in him became more pronounced. With his parents, he pretended to be back on track when really, he was disappointed by how slowly he was recovering both physically and academically. He devoted all his spare time to lessons, growing increasingly fatigued. Lack of exercise and insomnia made things worse. He began drinking more at night to help him relax and re-energize, but his highs were short-lived, and he began to suffer from acute anxiety. After missing several rehearsals, the conductor took him aside to find out what was happening and issue a warning. "I'm never going to catch up anyway," Xiu said, "I've tried my best, but it isn't good enough." Eventually, Xiu found his way but learned he had to put boundaries in his relationship with his parents to overcome his perfectionism.

Childhood Trauma

Grand expectations are not the worst things our parents can throw at us. A parent's abandonment or abuse can cause lifelong suffering and pain. But even this can be overcome. Humans are wondrous at healing and growing against the odds.

Our parents can inadvertently cause trauma in our childhoods by becoming ill or even passing away; by sending us away to a boarding school we hate; or by getting divorced and potentially triggering feelings of emotional and physical instability for the child, although not all divorces have this outcome. Trauma can even result from events that later bring joy, such as moving to another country or the birth of a sibling who changes the status quo.

Before twelve-year-old Emma's parents divorced, they fought about everything, including her. Instead of realizing their fight was never about her, Emma started to try and keep her parents happy. Her mother was often angry with her father for being too lenient with her, letting her get away with not doing her chores, not checking her homework was done, and allowing her to stay up late at night. Her father felt her mother was too hard on her and did not give her enough free time in which to play and enjoy her childhood. Emma would try to appease both parents by representing herself to her mother as studious, diligent, and conscientious and to her father as carefree, rebellious, and fun-loving. She felt divided against herself sometimes but hoped if she kept each parent satisfied, at least there would be one less reason for conflict between them.

During one of her school holidays, Emma went away with a friend and her family on a beach holiday that she immensely enjoyed; worried about her parents, she put them out of her mind and had a break. When she returned, her father was no longer living at their house. He and Emma's mother explained they had *irreconcilable differences*; Emma felt that if only *she* had been able to reconcile them, and if only she had not been away on holiday and left them alone together, they would not have separated. Subconsciously, she blamed herself for their divorce for many years.

Even the most protective and careful of parents cannot always safeguard their children from trauma. There are other people and circumstances beyond the control of even those adults we trust and rely on to keep us safe.

War, for instance, displaces people, splitting up families and making children vulnerable to human trafficking. Awful crimes, from physical and sexual abuse to slavery and child labor, cause trauma. But less obvious traumas, however seemingly small to the adult perception, can also violate a child's sense of self. Bullying, for example, need not involve pushing and punching or insults and threats. We have all heard of cases of micro-aggressions against a child at school which, if consistent and repetitive, can destroy the mental health of the child and their families.

Gradually, traumatic experiences of varying degrees can build up, lowering self-esteem and driving us to feel we need to prove to ourselves and others we are worthy of love and acceptance.

Academic Pressures

Our school system often reinforces the idea perfection is desirable and attainable. Young people are exposed early to the importance of higher qualifications to obtain work that pays well and provides recognition. They compete with others for the same positions, and standing out a head above the rest is a sure way to succeed.

The academic grade system in most countries sets children up as young as four or five to compare their scholastic and intellectual performance to that of others. If they get a bad grade, teachers involve parents to help the child become aware of their shortcomings and perform better.

When Jo received 4 medals at an award ceremony in middle school, contrary to her school's best intentions, she suddenly felt uneasy. It may seem strange she would have disliked their celebration of her achievements. But she sensed how her fellow students stared at her with a mixture of admiration and envy. To her, the discs on ribbons seemed fake and unnecessary. She also noticed the awards and ceremony made her classmates feel bad about themselves, which hurt her more than the good feeling she felt from the awards. "Was the ceremony really necessary, she thought?" She was more than happy to have her teachers tell her she was doing well and to learn the skills and knowledge underlying all that *hoopla*.

Those who do not score high marks or win trophies in such academic systems, or who mature at a slower rate than their peers, may internalize they do not merit certain dreams or aspirations, when comparing themselves with those external benchmarks. They may settle too soon for lives they have not really chosen.

Social Media

Social media is now so mainstream it is one of the main ways we communicate and share information. However, online activity can eat away at our time spent with people we know in person. Previous generations had to learn social skills face-to-face, where there is no option to *edit* or *delete* one's comments; members of Gen Z have also socialized over the internet all their lives. Social media can be an excellent tool for connection; however, if left without guard rails, it can take over and become more harmful than good.

Studies show Gen Z tends to use social media that is video or image-based rather than textual (Garnham, 2022). Visual messages work differently from verbal or written ones. They carry a greater immediate emotional impact.

Like it or not, social media has shaped our culture's conception of beauty for the last 15 years. Social media does not necessarily cause body image concerns, but they have a strong association. Scientific research shows social networking sites are associated with body image and eating disorders (Holland & Tiggemann, 2016).

My social media account follows the news, psychology, philosophy, art, music, book reviews, cooking, and (to be honest) dogs. But my goddaughter's experience of the site is remarkably different: She follows celebrity gossip, trendy influencers, beauty products and popular music (and dogs too). When I compare my account with hers, it is as if we are on platforms that are worlds apart. How can I recommend the platform when my experience differs from hers? The Roman poet and philosopher Lucretius expresses this dilemma elegantly in *De Rerum Natura* (*On the Nature of Things*): "Ut quod ali cibus est aliis fiat acre venenum," or "That which to some is food, to others is rank poison" (Titus Lucretius Carus, 1743). Reputable news agents and publishers proofread, fact check, and take a certain amount of responsibility for the information they disseminate. However, social media platforms have thus far been mostly reluctant to take accountability for their shared content. So, it seems fair we hold ourselves accountable for any poison we consume.

My goddaughter insists she knows the difference between photoshopped images and reality. Nevertheless, even blatantly false reality fuels notions of physical perfection that objectify our bodies and skew our perceptions. Social media is rife with images of perfection. Filters and photoshopping applications (*apps*) allow people to tweak and alter their appearance in the posts they upload to social media platforms. This manipulation gives them an illusory sense of control over their self-image while simultaneously preoccupying them with it. The filters and apps support notions of beauty as smooth-skinned flawlessness that are unabashedly fake.

According to senior tech policy reporter for MIT Technology Review, Tate Ryan-Mosley (2021):

The face filters that have become commonplace across social media are perhaps the most widespread use of augmented reality. Researchers don't yet understand the impact that sustained use of augmented reality may have, but they do know there are real risks—and with face filters, young girls are the ones taking that risk. They are subjects in an experiment that will show how technology changes the way we form our identities, represent ourselves, and relate to others. And it's all happening without much oversight.

Social Media *Likes* affirm. If there are not enough of them, the app user can delete the post. In this way, they can cover up their perceived imperfection. Professor Thomas Curran teaches in the Department of Psychological and Behavioral Sciences at the London School of Economics and Political Science. According to his research, over 85% of adolescent girls compared themselves less favorably to others on social media, particularly concerning their body image (Libysn, 2022). Body dysmorphia, eating disorders like anorexia and bulimia, and self-harm can result from poor body image. Alarmingly, psychologists have found "robust cross-cultural evidence linking social media use to body image concerns, dieting, body surveillance, a drive for thinness and self-objectification in adolescents" (Simmons, 2016).

Even *body-positive* movements highlight the body as self-defining instead of other attributes. A 2019 study showed that although exposing women to body-positive content appeared to help them feel more satisfied with their bodies, even women who saw these images objectified themselves, focusing on appearance rather than skills or inner traits (Oakes, 2019).

It's not just girls. Social media accounts that promote fitness and bodybuilding convince boys their bodies should be more muscular. Another 2019 study of boys aged 11–18 showed a third of them were unhappy with their appearance (Hawgood, 2022). Many boys and men suffer from what has been named *bigorexia.* This body dysmorphic syndrome leads to excessive weightlifting, extreme dieting, and, often, harmful drugs like steroids to gain weight and muscle. Adolescents push themselves to develop the bodies of fully developed men before their young bodies are ready for it or impose on themselves perfectionistic ideals that are the stuff of superheroes and stereotypes.

In 2022, The Learning Network of The New York Times published teenagers' comments about how social media made them feel. Sam of Valley Stream North wrote he felt men were discouraged from sharing struggles or insecurities about their bodies and society has inaccurately pinned body image issues to just women. He says gender does not necessarily determine whether an individual suffers from poor body image. Boys like Julian and Augustine of Valley Stream North, James from Hoggard High School in Wilmington, and Jameson from Syracuse, New York, all say that social media does not negatively affect their body image, yet they feel motivated by social media to work out and get fit, suggesting they are aiming at self-improvement based on how they see their bodies and are not satisfied with them as they are.

Neuro Developmental Conditions

Attention Deficit Hyperactivity Disorder (ADHD) arises from neuro-divergence involving excessive inattention, hyperactivity, and impulsivity. It may seem counterintuitive to think of someone with ADHD as a perfectionist, but they often are.

People with ADHD have a history of being told to concentrate or focus more to align with so-called *normal* standards. After receiving a message repeatedly telling them they are not *up to par* and will not meet others' expectations on the first, second, or even third attempt, they may display perfectionism by compulsively redoing, postponing, or avoiding activities. They may also overcompensate for feelings of inadequacy brought about by ADHD and blame themselves for errors or limitations beyond their control.

Anxiety about details may cause those with ADHD to say the same thing or behave in the same way repeatedly. This is called *perseveration* and is different from *perseverance* (with which it shares the root word, meaning to *persist*) in that it indicates inflexible, purposeless fixation (Merriam-Webster, 2023). You may have noticed someone on the ADHD spectrum involuntarily repeating certain words, phrases, or actions, as if they are stuck on them. They may not know when to let something go, may not understand what exactly is required of them, and may not know where to begin when faced with a task.

Dr. J. Russell Ramsay, Director of the Adult ADHD Treatment and Research Program at the University of Pennsylvania and Professor of Clinical Psychology in Psychiatry, describes two types of perfectionism (2019):

1. Back-end perfectionism

Less common in adult ADHD but more common in the classical sense of perfectionism, back-end perfectionism sees incompletion of projects and failure to meet deadlines due to a sense they are not impeccable or could still be improved upon. Extensions are requested (often shamefully) and, when granted, form an obligation to deliver material of an even higher quality than initially intended.

2. Front-end perfectionism

More common among ADHD adults, this mindset creates rigid standards or preconditions that must be met to initiate the project in the first place. As adults with ADHD are more susceptible to distraction and dissuasion than others, there is some validity in having preconditions met, but front-end perfectionists may avoid and escape tasks altogether.

Perseveration is also different from obsessing, although it may look the same. Obsessiveness is more severe and is linked to Obsessive Compulsive Disorder (OCD). OCD is a mental health condition that occurs when obsessions (unwanted, intrusive thoughts, images, or urges that trigger intensely distressing feelings) result in compulsions or behaviors to get rid of obsessions and/or decrease distress (International OCD Foundation, 2023). Like ADHD, OCD has links with perfectionism (Drinks, n.d.). Excessive self-control and striving for perfection in children may indicate a risk for OCD (Dryden, 2018). While perfectionism does not lead to OCD, people with OCD are more inclined to show maladaptive perfectionist concerns.

As discussed above, the root causes of perfectionism do not provide an exhaustive list, and some or all may be present and interrelated. However, they are well-known triggers for a perfectionistic tendency. If you think you might be a perfectionist (as so many of us are), try the perfectionism quiz in the following chapter to find out where you lie on the perfectionist spectrum.

4

AM I A PERFECTIONIST?

The Great Gatsby by F. Scott Fitzgerald (1925) is one of the greatest stories ever told about a perfectionist. The idealistic Jay Gatsby changes who he is, rejecting his roots and reinventing himself to win the love of Daisy. If you have not read the novel yet, let me insert a spoiler alert here: Daisy, who embodies "Perfection" to Gatsby, turns out to be selfish, shallow, and dismally unworthy of him. Besides the narrator, the only person with any real connection to Gatsby is his father, who brags about his son's determination to improve himself. He shows the narrator a book in which, as a boy, Gatsby wrote down a strict daily schedule from 6 a.m.–9 p.m. The schedule included rising from bed, dumbbell exercises, wall-scaling, work, baseball and sports, practicing "elocution, poise and how to attain it" and studying inventions. This part of the book wrenches my heart because, as the narrator says, Gatsby was worth more than Daisy or any of the circles to which he was trying to belong.

If you are a perfectionist, you may be denying and even destroying your true self. Your perfectionist tendencies may be dishonoring and devaluing you much in the same way Gatsby's misled him. It is essential to take a hard look at your behavior and ask yourself whether you are doing yourself an injustice by demanding too much of yourself or letting others require too much of you.

By now, you at least have an idea about whether you are a perfectionist. The following quiz can give you further insight into your level of perfectionism and the dimension in which it most strongly exists. It can help you identify maladaptive perfectionistic tendencies you will want to overcome. This test is not a clinical test to diagnose perfectionistic traits and can only provide general guidance. For a clinical examination, please consult a certified practitioner.

TAKE THE MULTIDIMENSIONAL PERFECTIONISM QUIZ

How much of a perfectionist are you? The following test from Research Gate (2023) comprising questions, responses, and scores, will assist you in assessing to what extent you exhibit traits of self-oriented, socially prescribed, and other-oriented perfectionism (as discussed in Chapter 1).

Try not to give the "perfect" answer but rather the one that comes up first, even if you second-guess it afterward. Even if you are unsure about the answer, you will hit an estimate that will give you a reliable indication of where you fit in. Once you see how the test works, you can ask yourself related questions and gauge where your responses place you regarding your perfectionism.

Read each statement and choose a number most indicative of your opinion from 1–5 where:

1 is *never*
2 is *rarely*
3 is *sometimes*
4 is *often*
5 is *always*

Section A

Statement:

- I obsess over details.
- I check and recheck work before deciding it is finished.
- I get upset when I feel criticized.
- I could never meet adults' expectations when I was growing up.
- My home and workspace must be meticulously organized.
- I avoid tasks I might not be good at.
- If I don't continuously succeed, people won't respect me.
- It's difficult to make decisions.
- I often second-guess myself after making a decision.
- I am mortified if I make mistakes.
- I worry more than most.
- The time and effort I put into my work negatively affects my family and/or social life.
- I would be devastated to miss a deadline.
- My perfectionism is preventing me from living the life I would like to lead.

Total Score:

Section B

Statement:

- I worry about what others think of me.
- I want to be liked.
- I am careful of what I say so I make the right impression on others.
- I struggle to say "No," especially without offering a viable excuse.
- I feel guilty for taking time for myself.
- It's hard to ask for what I want.
- I avoid conflict or confrontational situations.
- It is too difficult for me to complain about bad service: I would rather just let it be, even when I know I am right.
- I feel anxious at the prospect of someone thinking ill of me or disliking me.
- Public speaking is extremely stressful for me.
- I won't be seen in public unless I am presentable.
- I am reluctant to meet new people. etc.
- Social situations unnerve me, and so I avoid them.
- I feel inferior to those who are more successful, more intelligent, funnier, more attractive, etc., than me.

- People will despise me if I am foolish or make a mistake.

Total Score:

Section C

Statement:

- I've been called overly critical and judgmental.
- I've been told I'm too fussy.
- I can become preoccupied with others' shortcomings.
- It takes a lot to earn my trust.
- I've been told I do not give others the benefit of the doubt and expect the worst of them.
- It irritates me when others make mistakes.
- People often seem nervous when I am with them.
- I've been called controlling.
- I am wary of being influenced, manipulated, bossed around, or controlled.
- I am vigilant against being taken advantage of or hustled.
- People who care for one another should not disagree.

- I prefer to manage entirely by myself rather than delegate or ask for help.
- If you want something done well, you should do it yourself. Others are unlikely to do as good a job as you.
- It irks me when others don't measure up to my standards.
- I hate to be interrupted.

Total Score:

Use the following to calculate how you score in each area:

15–26 Little or no tendency
27–38 Mild to moderate tendency
39-50 Moderate to strong tendency
51-62 Strong to very strong tendency
63-75 Very strong tendency

Each section of the above quiz relates to one of the three types of perfectionism discussed in Chapter 1: self-oriented perfectionism (SOP), socially prescribed perfectionism (SPP), and other-oriented perfectionism (OOP).

If you score around 50 and above in Section A (SOP), you likely impose impossibly lofty standards on yourself. Fear of failure, and the inability to meet your expectations of yourself, may lead to self-loathing, depression, and despair. If you stop to think about how you treat yourself, you may realize you would never treat anyone you cared about in the same way. While you think being hard on yourself is a way to succeed in life, it may hold you back. Negative self-talk, self-recrimination, and forcing yourself to perform better may be causing you to feel divided against yourself: There is a part of you that knows you do not deserve to be treated this way and wants unconditional self-acceptance. You may find yourself using substances such as alcohol as a way of self-soothing to relieve your body from the stress you are subjecting it to with your constant vigilance and self-denial. You may see rest and pleasure as luxuries you put off until you feel you have earned or deserve them.

If your score is below 50 in this area, do not worry about having low standards or being an under-achiever; as we have mentioned, and contrary to widespread belief, perfectionism does not equal excellence but can inhibit and prevent people from reaching their potential or achieving their goals.

A high score in Section B (SPP) indicates you feel held to the impossibly demanding standards of others. Certain people make you feel as if you need to be better than you are or as if you are not enough, such as your parents, life partner, boss, or even your online fans and followers, if you have them. The admiration of others may confirm that loving attention is correlated to achievement. Even people who are well-loved and supported by their friends and family may feel they should aim for the stars; our society perpetuates the idea that special people—those with extraordinary skills or striking looks, for example—matter more in the world than ordinary people.

As you exert yourself to fulfill the expectations of others, whether they be explicit, implied, or even imaginary, you may find yourself lonely, isolated, and swamped by low self-esteem and social anxiety. Fear of ostracism and humiliation may prevent you from trying anything new. You may also feel anger and resentment against certain people or society, especially those in authority over you.

Section C (OOP) covers perfectionists with unrealistic standards of others, often leading to problematic relationships at work and home. If you score high in this area, those around you tend to avoid you to shield themselves from your criticism and requirements for perfection. They may hide aspects of their lives from you to shield them from your scrutiny and disapproval. They may say you expect too much from them. This may surprise you, especially if you are also an SOP who asks nothing more than what you ask of yourself. If those closest to you do not excel, it may be an indictment on you. A parent, for example, may feel that when their child fails or struggles, it is due to poor parenting. A husband whose wife goes through a period of personal loss or hardship may feel her suffering reflects poorly on him as a husband. "It's not always about you," we may have heard people say.

It is normal to identify with all three types of perfectionism. Those questions where you scored 4 or 5 on are worth thinking about. When perfectionistic characteristics cause relationship problems, jeopardize work or recreational activity, or interfere with your enjoyment of life, you can choose to make a change.

Having discussed some of the signs of perfectionism above, let us take a deeper look into how perfectionism reveals itself, the havoc it can wreak, and—importantly —how you can identify your brand of perfectionism in your life.

5

HOW PERFECTIONISM SHOWS UP IN OUR LIVES

Once we have examined the signs of perfectionism, you will have a clearer idea of where you stand on the perfectionist spectrum. Then we will move on in the final chapters of this book to techniques, tools, and steps that will help you overcome your perfectionism. Your perfectionism can ruin your life and negatively impact how others relate to you. Perfectionism increases the risk for various psychological disorders, such as eating disorders, anxiety disorders, and depression (Egan, Wade & Shafran, 2010).

ANXIETY AND STRESS

Social anxiety is common, as most people fear a negative evaluation in social situations. We worry about our social skills in particular contexts more than others. For instance, I have more social anxiety at an official function attended by my peers, especially if I must give a presentation or speech, than when meeting colleagues for drinks after work on a Friday.

While in the grip of perfectionism, I used to work late on Fridays as if it were any other night of the week and declined invitations to socialize. I wanted to pour every spare minute into my work and viewed mixing events as a waste of time. I was concerned about people with whom I had to work getting to know me too well and preferred to keep a wall of professionalism between us. As I changed and began to make friends at work, I realized what I'd been missing: Work friends bring a richness and joy to the workplace I did not know could exist. Instead of depleting me, they assisted and supported me emotionally and with practical issues. I have also found a generosity of spirit in myself that is much easier to live with than the cut-throat, competitive mentality with which my career began. We can improve perfectionism not only with concerted effort but with maturity.

Overestimating social standards and underestimating one's ability to meet them are two main factors that lead to individual social anxiety (Hoffman, 2007). Studies suggest perfectionism is more likely to cause individuals to perceive stress in their lives (Wang et al., 2022). Perceived stress (i.e., stress of which one is conscious or aware) predicts an elevated level of social anxiety.

When social anxiety becomes extreme and insurmountable, it becomes social anxiety disorder (SAD): an acute, unending, and uncontrollable fear of being critically observed by others.

DEPRESSION

A recent study by psychologist Katarina Rnic reveals all perfectionism traits or all dimensions of perfectionism result in greater depression severity due to social disconnection, leading to social hopelessness and loneliness (Rnic et al., 2021).

My perfectionism led to bouts of depression. I lost interest in everything but work, and even that eventually became dull. My sleep patterns changed; at first, I needed less sleep, and then, all I wanted to do was sleep as I caved into lethargy and fatigue. "I'm so tired," I would repeatedly say, trying to explain why I felt the way I did. I also lost weight without trying and found it increasingly difficult to concentrate. When I finally accepted I was depressed, which did not fit my narrative of perfection, I could ask for support and assistance and set out on the road to recovery that involved a new narrative of self-compassion.

IMPOSTOR SYNDROME

The social phenomenon that is Impostor Syndrome (IS) has varied definitions, as it is not considered a clinical diagnosis or disorder. Clinical psychologists Pauline Rose Clance and Suzanne Imes developed the concept in the '70s, defining it as "a psychological experience of intellectual and professional fraudulence" (Page, 2022). Clance points out people with IS believe their success is only due to breaks and courage; in the ABC Framework of Success, in which A is for ability, B for breaks, and C for courage, the ability is perceived as missing by someone with IS (Clance, 1985).

A friend of mine endured IS for over a year after being required to deliver a presentation to his department of peers in marketing. He prepared for weeks in advance and had sleepless nights leading up to it. Afterward, several colleagues complimented him, saying he was clear, concise, and thorough, which was not the feedback he had expected. After all the concentration and effort, he still felt his presentation could have been more complex and strayed from the topic. He also remembered every single "Um" he uttered while giving it. He explained his colleagues' response by telling himself they could see his distress, felt sorry for him, and were just being nice. In reality, he told himself, they thought he was ignorant of the business and mediocre at presenting.

He still felt relieved because he thought he had gotten away with it this time; but he worried how long his luck would hold out. The more attention and praise he received, month by month, served only to increase the sensation he would ultimately be exposed as a fraud. He felt self-doubt and worried about letting down his team at work. This drove him to attain even greater heights as he overcompensated for his inadequacy. Eventually, he accepted his co-workers' congratulations as genuine by doing inner work with some of the tools we will discuss later in this book. Learning to acknowledge his contribution to the company as tangible helped him overcome IS.

Research shows a strong link between IS, self-oriented perfectionism/SOP, and socially prescribed perfectionism/SPP (Pannhausen et al., 2020). Studies also show IS (also called impostorism) is closely related to low self-esteem, which, hypothetically, is a precondition of IS (Cokley et al., 2018).

Schubert and Bowker (2017) reported impostorism negatively correlates with self-esteem and positively correlates with self-esteem instability. They emphasized the critical role of self-esteem problems in impostorism, suggesting people with low self-esteem are particularly vulnerable to impostor feelings. Neureiter and Traut-Mattausch (2016) also hypothesized low self-esteem was a precondition of impostorism and found low self-esteem correlates with prominent levels of impostor feelings.

EATING DISORDERS AND POOR BODY IMAGE

Media has entrenched a notion among people that power resides in appearance. To make the most of that power, one should be a certain age, weight, shape, look, etc. Perfection equated with beauty causes many women and men to develop eating disorders. However, the root of eating disorders is more complicated than that; the feeling of being able to control what one puts in the body gives the illusion of control over one's life.

There are many kinds of eating disorders, but the following are two of the most common (Petre, 2019):

Anorexia nervosa

Symptoms of anorexia nervosa include restricted eating; fear of gaining weight even when underweight; a distorted body image; an almost irrational desire for thinness; self-esteem dependent on body weight or shape; obsessive-compulsive behavior relating to food (keeping track of every calorie in daily food intake and picking out and discarding certain foods from a prepared meal, for example).

Bulimia nervosa

Often described as the other side of the coin to anorexia nervosa and related to the same obsessive-compulsive behavior toward food (especially binge-eating and purging), self-esteem influenced by body weight or shape, bulimia nervosa differs from anorexia in that there are no significant fluctuations in body weight.

Karen Carpenter was a singer and drummer in the popular 70's American band, The Carpenters, with her brother, Richard, playing piano and singing backup vocals. She became famous for her unique voice at age 21 when the hit *Close to You* reached No. 1 on the US charts. A review of a new documentary titled Karen Carpenter: Starving for Perfection (2023) relates how, when she passed away in 1983 at the age of 32 after suffering from heart failure due to anorexia, her death prompted widespread media coverage of the eating disorder for the first time (Byrne, 2023). Little was known at the time about the condition. The review mentions Karen lost so much weight toward the end of her life; her audiences gasped when she entered the stage because of how dramatically she had changed in such a short time.

According to the documentary, Karen idolized her brother, Richard, who was regarded as a musical child prodigy and adored by the family. Her anorexia seems to have been triggered by "a quest for [musical] perfection that carried over [to other aspects] in her life." Karen was also said to have suffered from external pressure from the media to be the "It" girl of the moment and to reflect a feminine ideal she did not identify with. Although it was her singing people praised, screenwriter Randy L. Schmidt says (Byrne, 2023):

> She was a drummer first and considered herself a drummer who just happened to sing, which is crazy to think about because she was incredibly talented as a vocalist. She got her start as a jazz drummer, and that's what she wanted to do. The voice was really an accident. She just accidentally had this voice that needed no training — just a refining. She was only 15, 16, when the voice started to emerge.
>
> If her voice came so naturally, she may have thought it had less to do with her ability than drumming, where her genuine interest lay.
>
> Having the role of a perfect woman with an ideal

voice forced on her and trying to meet others' expectations without the freedom to explore her true self may have led to perfectionism that ultimately killed her.

A study of women with eating disorders such as anorexia nervosa, bulimia nervosa, and others shows that (Petersson et al., 2017):

- Although patients with eating disorders direct their perfectionistic striving to physical appearance, their primary aim is not to obtain a perfect body but rather to obtain order, self-control, and top performance.
- Although they regard perfection as unattainable and exhausting, they adopt it as a strategy to handle feelings of low self-esteem and anxiety.

You will remember that perfectionistic strivings, often considered a positive side of self-oriented perfectionism, involve setting demanding standards for oneself. Perfectionist concerns include being critical of oneself and worrying about what others think. Research finds perfectionistic strivings have more to do with eating disorders than perfectionist concerns, which have more to do with depression and anxiety disorders (Rozental, 2020). This research gives credence to what Dr. Hewitt has said all along: even the side of perfectionism we associate with self-improvement can be dark and destructive.

People with poor body image can feel detached from their bodies. They may feel as if they disappear into their heads and lose touch with their bodies; they may not even want to have bodies. They may avoid looking at themselves in the mirror or forget their appearance.

Others may spend time staring at their reflection without seeing themselves realistically. They may have dysmorphic body disorder, focusing excessively on one feature or aspect of their bodies they do not feel comfortable with. They may obsess over parts of their bodies they think should be different.

If you have a poor body image, you might:

- Try not to see your body.
- Wish you had another body or nobody at all.
- Need to make sure that your body is there or as you remember it to be by checking it in the mirror or examining it.
- Pick at your skin or self-harm by hurting yourself.
- Hide away behind make-up, outfits, or loose-fitting clothing.

- Decline taking part in physical activities and avoid being seen by other people.
- Say negative things about the way you look.
- Feel strong, negative emotions about your body or parts of it.
- Undervalue the almost miraculous way in which your body works.
- Focus more on what your body cannot do instead of appreciating all it can do.

You can help yourself like your body by focusing on how it enables you to live in the world. Does it carry you from one place to another, show you things, and explore different flavors, textures, and sensations? Think of the people who love and relate to you through your body: How magical it is to look into their eyes or hug them.

PROCRASTINATION

When people procrastinate, they postpone or delay doing what they mean to do, putting it off for later. Aiming for nothing short of perfection produces anxiety; people procrastinate to ease their anxiety but end up developing even more stress, forming a vicious circle.

Perfectionism can lead to indecisiveness due to being wary of making a mistake, however small or inconspicuous a mistake might be. Making a mistake about something insignificant may shake confidence about making more critical decisions. Suppose I doubt myself to make a choice, commit or follow through, or my choices are made for me anyway. In that case, I may be more inclined to procrastinate than if I feel capable, confident, and in charge of my direction in life.

There is a person I know named Iris, who is a gifted artist. She writes beautifully, draws, and paints with a sensitive, attentive eye and an experienced, loose, expressive hand. She makes it look easy—the art-making part, at least. She works hard and, like many artists, struggles for recognition and funds, concentrating on her art in her spare time after office work.

She shared that she has a recurring nightmare that she is trying to set up an exhibition in graduate school. "Those years should have been among the best of my life," she mused, "But they still fill me with dread. I barely scraped through. I remember working through the night trying to throw something together that could pass as art because I had never gotten around to whatever I'd planned. My lecturers must have thought I was disinterested. But I was clinically depressed. I felt as if art was all that mattered to me, all I wanted to do with my life, and it was just too much for me. I didn't want to try and fail." Knowing how much was required of her to become the artist she wanted to be and how much she would lose should she fail, she kept stalling, bunking, and not showing up. She still feels guilty about not making the most of her studies.

"I remember how I couldn't decide whether to work on paper or cloth, one time," she adds, "I went back and forth trying this kind of paper, that kind of cloth until all I had were piles of half-worked panels. I sewed them together at the end and displayed them like that even though I had intended to make something quite different and better." She pauses momentarily and laughs, "When viewers said the piece was good art, I started to panic!" It can be extra stressful for a perfectionist to feel that others don't get it, that they are wrong about their abilities, or do not understand what the perfectionist wants.

ALL-OR-NOTHING THINKING

All-or-nothing or black-and-white thinking fuels perfectionism and its cousin, procrastination. All-or-nothing thinkers see themselves and situations in terms of extremes. They commonly use the words always and never, even though it is rare for things always or never to happen. I'm always messing up, they may say, basing self-recrimination on tumultuous feelings instead of reason. If they kept a record of how often they messed up instead of managing, they would see they were coping well overall.

All-or-nothing thinking sounds like:

"If I can't do this well, it's not worth doing."

They can apply this condition to anything — from writing a eulogy, taking up ceramics, or vacuuming the carpet. Some things matter more than others, and only some things must be done well. Anticipating they will not do something well prevents them from starting or causes them to give up too quickly.

Some endeavors require persistence and may go wrong before they go right. I remember learning this when I painted a room in my house. I prepared thoroughly, washing the wall with sugar soap; sanding and scraping off loose paint around cracks, filling, and smoothing holes; masking the skirtings, door, and window; comparing color swatches and samples; laying out a drop sheet, brushes, rollers, and paint trays, and setting up a ladder. I thought most of the work was done. I cut the edges and rolled on the first layer of paint. It looked terrible to me, uneven, with blotches and bare patches. But I knew more than one coat would be required, so I went around the room again, noticing the paint was running out faster than I expected. It was also a much messier job than I expected, and I had to keep wiping up drops and spatters that missed the drop sheet and landed on the floor. I got paint in my hair and all over my hands, arms, and T-shirt. My muscles ached after hours of climbing up and down the ladder. By the end of the day, when I thought I would have a finished room, I had only one half-finished room and could only continue once I had returned to the store for more paint the following day.

By the end of the next day, I finished painting the room, but not without seriously doubting whether I would complete the job and be satisfied with it. It took much longer and more out of me than I thought when I first imagined doing it, and the walls passed through several stages of incompletion before they began to look solid and neat again. The following day, when the light was better, I noticed a few streaks and areas that needed touching up. I probably wouldn't have done it if I had known what a challenging task it would be. Still, I loved how it turned out and was immensely proud of myself for pushing through.

"I'm not ready to do this yet."

Waiting for conditions to be "right" or to feel prepared before undertaking something might mean it never gets done. Another way to approach a mammoth task is to jump right in and learn how to get through it as one goes along. Being thrown in at the deep end, my father used to call it, and he would say, "You either sink or swim." But this analogy may sound a bit intimidating, as is the other one about "jumping off of a cliff and building one's wings on the way down." Approaching a task in smaller sections rather than all at once can be less scary than seeing the entire project scope — all at once. Even though planning is helpful, it cannot replace implementing one's ideas as they develop.

Setting out with only a rough plan might terrify a perfectionist who prefers to have every contingency provided for. Still, it can also free a person to get started and move from one step to another instead of trying to plan the entire process. This is the attitude you will have when reading the last chapters of this book. Overcoming perfectionism may seem like something one needs all one's energy for, but with patience and consistency, you can achieve it.

"This is too hard. Something's missing."

Feeling that an essential ingredient is missing (such as self-esteem) may hold you back when all you need is already there in you.

Iris, the brilliant artist, used to think she would be a better artist if she could afford better equipment and materials. One day, an artist friend invited her to use their very well-equipped studio and help herself to any of the paints and other mediums she wanted. Iris enjoyed herself but still felt as if there was a missing ingredient. She reflected on when she could not afford new materials and how she still made art from found objects, scraps of fabric and embroidery thread, and old household enamel. "Rauschenberg's Combine paintings inspired me," she says. "There was a time when he also was too poor to buy art materials." She realized he had turned his lack to his advantage, and she had too. Being challenged by limitations helped her to be more creative, in a way. She thanked the artist who had been so generous with his studio; but she was most grateful for the epiphany that it wasn't her lack of resources holding her back.

"Someone else could do this just as well or better with half the effort."

Although this might be true for some things, and delegating specific tasks is standard and even wise sometimes, there are certain experiences and processes that change us for the better in ways we could not have predicted when we undertake them. Why would anyone leave something worth doing (even badly) to someone else? It is not only what gets done that matters, or how it gets done, but what doing it does to us and how it shapes and informs us.

"If this doesn't work out, I don't know what I'll do!"

Finding oneself in a place or situation one didn't anticipate can be unnerving, especially if it is a dead end.

Like when a family in Ohio spent around $50,000 planting citrus trees on their farm, only to have the whole crop fail, and the trees cut down. But in the face of a lemon of an investment, they decided to graft new specimens onto the old rootstock of the felled trees, and they would not lose hope. The excitement of what might still grow gave them a new and entertaining topic of conversation at dinner, and it was a project they were all into. The accusation that hope is misleading is sad: Only false hope is false, but hope aligned to one's values and true intention leads to courage, tenacity, and breakthrough.

"I'll never forgive them for making that mistake."

We have all heard of families where members no longer speak to one another. Some of the most vicious lawsuits are filed by one family member against another. Hurt can run deep and threaten every good memory or prospect of reconciliation.

Even seemingly minor offenses can tear people apart. I remember hearing about two sisters who fell out over a porcelain dish set their mother promised them when she died. The eldest ended up keeping the set, and her sister begrudged her to such an extent they fought and refused to speak again for years. When the older sister suddenly passed away unexpectedly, her sister realized, too late, this intransigent attitude had cost them significantly more than any porcelain dish set was worth.

Deciding to never or always do something makes you a shadow of who you are, limiting your possibilities by holding you to your extremes.

"That one slip-up ruined everything."

Cancel culture holds people accountable or punishes and ostracizes them when they do or say something that is considered by society as inappropriate or unacceptable. Even the work of artists like Picasso or Gauguin has faced cancel culture scrutiny because they have been judged retroactively by today's sociopolitical moral standards. We have seen a spectrum of public figures, some who have committed egregious acts, some who have made a gaff considered politically incorrect during a live interview, face career-damaging consequences for their mistakes.

Although cancel culture outcomes may be appropriate for some situations, the bigger point here is that categorical all-or-nothing thinking denies the myriad complexities, many different contexts, subtle gradations, nuances, changes, cycles, and seasons of life. It can lead to anxiety, hopelessness, self-defeating behavior, and depression.

RUMINATION

Cognitive perseveration or chronic overthinking refers to continual, involuntary negative thoughts about past or future events and includes worry and rumination.

According to Xie et al. (2019), the Perfectionism Cognition Theory (PCT) provides a theoretical explanation of how perfectionism works cognitively (in conscious intellectual activity such as thinking, reasoning, or remembering) with an emphasis on cognitive perseveration. It finds that:

- Perfectionism and cognitive perseveration are related.
- Self-oriented perfectionism (SOP) and socially prescribed perfectionism (SPP) involve cognitive perseveration, ruminating on mistakes, past events, and social comparisons aggravating anxiety and stress in perfectionists.
- Cognitive perseveration can mentally and physically affect perfectionists, reducing mental capacity and causing physical exhaustion.

Worry and rumination share similarities, such as negative, repetitive thought processes, but worry is more future-oriented and rumination more past-oriented; worry focuses on events and rumination on feelings, and women tend to ruminate more than men (Xie et al. 2019). When we worry, we are afraid of what might happen in the future; trying to anticipate future events, and imagining futures removes us from participation in the present moment, which is the only space we most fully exist in, here and now. When we ruminate, we want to make sense of what happened in the past; We try to make peace with the past by re-living it in our mind, again removing ourselves from the present moment. We think rumination will prevent whatever is troubling us from happening again. People who ruminate may do so to try to work through their problems. Still, rumination is different from problem-solving, as thoughts go around and around without resolution or closure.

While rumination can sap the pleasure out of our waking life, worry keeps us awake at night, panicking about all sorts of things, most of which never happen.

RELATIONSHIP PROBLEMS

Perfectionism harms relationships. Many people think their perfectionism is their business and no one else's. It becomes others' business when it affects the quality of communication and obstructs intimacy between people.

A perfectionist's grand expectations of themselves and self-criticism can lead to unhappiness and a need for continual emotional support and reassurance. A perfectionist's expectations and criticism of a partner can lead to feelings of mutual disappointment and neglect, and resentment in the partner who wants to be loved, accepted, and appreciated for who they are. Perfectionists may hide their flaws, and those who are tired of being criticized by them may also compromise emotional intimacy. Perfectionists can be intolerant and inflexible and find it hard to relax and have fun, which can harm relationships.

When I was small, my father seemed perfect to me, and I adored him; likewise, he expressed nothing but affection and approval for me. But as I grew older, I began to differentiate myself from my parents, as one does to become independent. Perhaps because I had been so influenced by my dad and close to him, I made an especially concerted effort to push him away. It was also because I regarded his perception of me as perfect, inaccurate, and annoying. I suspected he would no longer honestly like me if I changed and did not follow his rules or take special note of his opinions. We went through a rocky period of discord and testing. However, as I settled into adulthood, we reconciled, and I still laugh about my stubborn attitude and rebellious adolescence. I wasn't exactly "bad," but I called him out a lot and expected him to continue to measure up to my ideal even though I refused to measure up to his.

Superficial relationships can have their place and time, but it is our most intimate relationships that need to be nurtured and maintained.

When Letitia got married, her husband thought her perfect in every way. She was beautiful, ambitious, and kind. But as their marriage progressed, whenever Letitia expressed opinions or desires that contradicted his, they would find themselves in an argument. "It's as if you want to father me," she said to him one day when she thought she couldn't take anymore. "You keep telling me what I should and shouldn't do, asking me what I've accomplished today, giving me instructions. This isn't what I married you for. I wanted to be in a balanced partnership with you, where I would feel equally as important as you are. Instead, you seem to think of me as an inept child."

Whenever she tried to tell him about worries or concerns, he would offer a solution rather than listen and empathize with her. He was surprised she saw his advice as unhelpful. As a perfectionist, it was difficult for him to concede she could have a different approach to life than his that might make more sense to her. Marriage counseling encouraged respectful dialogue, and they could move forward, admitting they did not want to be carbon copies of one another but enjoyed their differences. Letitia and her husband had issues with perfectionism they learned to recognize and address.

ASSESS YOUR AREAS OF PERFECTIONISM

Before moving on to practical ways in which you can overcome your perfectionism, it is helpful to identify specific areas in life where we have exhibited perfectionistic tendencies. Here is a table to assist you, adapted from Overcoming Perfectionism (Roz Shafran et al., 2018):

Step 1: Copy the table on a page with enough space to work with. If you cannot write it out at this stage, consider the areas and whether you have perfectionist tendencies. Feel free to add any areas not included in the table.

Step 2: Highlight each area in which you think you have perfectionism.

Step 3: What thoughts do you have about each area? Write what your mind tells you.

Step 4: What perfectionist behavior do you display in each area? Consider what you do or what actions you take.

Step 5: How does engaging in these thoughts and behaviors make you feel? Write about your emotions, even if they do not make much sense.

Area of Perfectionism	Thoughts	Behaviors	Feelings
Example: Physical fitness	*I should exercise so my heart rate is in the range of 50–85% of my maximum heart rate for at least 20 minutes daily.*	*For the first few days, I push myself to exceed my goal, but then exercise drops from daily to weekly to not at all, and I criticize and chastise myself.*	*I feel disappointed in myself. The prospect of starting over seems more difficult than when I first set out, as if I am worse off. Regular exercise is not good enough: It must be daily or not at all. I am angry with myself. I feel like a slob.*
Physical fitness			
Appearance			
Body shape			
Weight			
Eating			
Health			
Hygiene			
Social skills			
Hosting/ entertaining			
Family relationships			
Parenting			

Intimate relationships			
Sexual performance			
Artistic skills (visual, musical, etc.)			
Sports ability			
Academic achievement			
Work success			
Wealth			
House cleanliness			
Organizing/ making lists/order			
Checking locks/ turning off switches			

Table: Areas of perfection and associated thoughts, behavior, and feelings

Now that you have given some thought to how perfectionism shows up and what you do and feel about it, let us look at effective ways to counteract those tendencies.

6

COGNITIVE BEHAVIOR
EXERCISES

Michelle is a college student who pays for her college expenses with money she earns as a part-time cashier at a local clothing boutique. She is predisposed to perfectionistic concerns about her ability in mathematics and managing her finances.

During her first month as a cashier, she accidentally gave a customer a $10 bill instead of $20 in change. The customer realized she had been shortchanged and asked for the outstanding amount. Realizing her error, Michelle apologized profusely, blushing and light-headed with embarrassment. It wasn't the first time she had miscalculated change. As a server while studying in school, she sometimes had to pay in from her tips due to insufficient takings when cashing up at the end of the night. She felt as if the customer could see her whole history of blunders.

The customer tried to ease her discomfort as she smiled and took the $10 with a cheerful, "No worries!" but it ruined her day. For weeks afterward, she replayed the event over in her mind. How had she made such a dumb mistake? She asked herself. Had she been careless or distracted, or was she not smart enough to give accurate change to customers? From then on, Michelle reactively became anxious whenever a customer paid with cash.

Nervous about making a mistake, she would triple-check the change she gave each customer, counting coins and bills several times. Sometimes customers found her behavior amusing; she interpreted their smiles as smirks of disapproval. They occasionally inspected the change themselves with a suspicious side-ways glance, suggesting her self-doubt had caused them to doubt her too. Their doubt, in turn, increased her insecurity.

Her preoccupation with this issue reached a point where Michelle wanted to quit. However, she needed the income to continue her studies. It affected her self-esteem; Michelle asked herself how she would ever run her own business as she wanted to do after graduating if she could not cope with being a cashier.

When she confided in a close friend about this, he told her to "chill out" and "stop trying so hard," but this was not advice she could use. She decided to approach a trusted college counselor who recommended cognitive behavioral therapy.

The therapist suggested doing some cognitive behavior exercises to challenge her beliefs about her behavior and its impact on customers. By intentionally following a different course of action when she had to give change in cash, Michelle found she could provide the correct change reliably without rechecking it and learned to expect a few mistakes without seeing them as portents of a doomed career. As her anxiety eased, she again started to enjoy her work as a cashier; Her positive attitude toward her studies returned, and she felt hopeful again about becoming an entrepreneur who would one day have a design label.

The therapy that helped Michelle with her issue is called cognitive therapy or cognitive behavioral therapy (CBT) and is defined as "psychotherapy that combines cognitive therapy and behavior therapy by identifying faulty or maladaptive patterns of thinking, emotional response, or behavior and substituting them with desirable patterns of thinking, emotional response, or behavior." (Merriam-Webster, 2023). CBT works on the premise that one's mental, emotional, and physical states are interdependent. It involves talk therapy to help people manage problems in these areas. It is usually conducted in several 30–60-minute sessions every one or two weeks with a therapist who helps the patient analyze problematic beliefs or behaviors and develop alternative ones (NHS, 2021).

Michelle believed if she didn't recheck her calculations when handling cash, she would let another mistake slip through. She thought she was preventing errors by counting the coins and bills thrice. The behavior experiment involved repeated checking every two days, not daily, and otherwise checking only once, writing down her feelings immediately after and then an hour after giving the customer their change. Although Michelle felt checking helped reassure her when she first started experimenting, she realized that behavior did not ease her anxiety but increased it. Notes made during the experiment also revealed checking the change more than once did not make her feel more confident an hour later, and she had not shortchanged the customer. Michelle was surprised she was less worried about accuracy in her calculations on days when she checked the change only once and after an hour after interacting with the customer.

CBT trains people to disrupt destructive patterns by changing how they act based on what they think about something. It often proves to patients that they are forced to react specifically to mental or emotional impetus, and healthier behavior indicates healthier ways of thinking and feeling. It is consistently proven to be an effective therapy in the treatment of perfectionism. It helps the person to conceptualize their perfectionism and treat it with techniques such as preventing repeated checking, conducting behavioral tests to examine beliefs, refuting the ones that are dysfunctional, and introducing activities unrelated to accomplishments (Rozental, 2020). In experiments, current behaviors are tested against new ones that hopefully lead to healthier beliefs and feelings.

The sound of words like experiment and experimentation can intimidate people as they conjure up ideas about labs and scientists. However, behavioral "experimentation" is a self-led way of testing whether your behavior makes sense and works for you. Behavioral "experiments" help people who are concerned about being controlled by their perfectionism test whether the predictions that compel them to behave a certain way are, in fact, valid.

The primary goal of a behavioral experiment is to gather information to test the logic of what you do and why you do it. We all act according to cognitive biases or beliefs. We make predictions about the consequences of our behavior, whether we are conscious of it or not. The experiments provide helpful information about your opinions and predictions, how they affect your behavior, and whether the belief is accurate and the behavior beneficial.

An essential part of a behavioral experiment is manipulating or purposely altering something in your behavior to see what happens. The experiment should be systematic and deliberate, describing the usual belief and resulting behavior, deciding how the behavior will be different during the experiment, and recording the outcome of the behavior change. Behavior experiments ultimately test the complete accuracy of your beliefs and biases and prove you have a choice regarding how to respond to perceived pressures.

There is no right way to do a behavioral experiment. Think of it as a tool to help you analyze your specific perfectionist tendencies by gathering evidence that will either confirm or disprove the beliefs that motivate your behavior. Your ideas may be so entrenched that you've never questioned them before. You owe it to yourself and others to see how well-founded they are, if they truly serve you, and to offer an alternative course of action more beneficial to you. If you would like professional support with CBT, you can consult a licensed therapist who specializes in this therapy.

WORKSHEET FOR BEHAVIORAL EXPERIMENTS

Below is a worksheet adapted from Overcoming Perfectionism (Roz Shafran et al., 2018) to assist you in conducting simple behavioral experiments. Document in writing each of the below steps so you can keep track of the thoughts, behaviors, alternate experimental behavior, and outcomes to run these successfully:

Step 1: Identify your belief.

Step 2: State what you think happens in general terms when your actions do not support your belief.

Step 3: Decide to experiment in a specific situation by modifying your usual behavior and state what you think will happen, specifically, in as much detail as possible.

Step 4: Do it. Be deliberately imperfect in the specific situation you have in mind. Do something in a way you would not usually do it or do not think should be done — in a less-than-perfect way.

Step 5: Describe the results of your experiment: What happened, in detail, and monitor your anxiety levels at set intervals (you could use a scale from 1–10 where 1 is low and 10 extremely high).

Step 6: Compare the results in Step 5 to what you thought would happen (Step 3), and consider whether your belief was disproved or not, in this instance, and whether your prediction was accurate and to what extent.

Step 7: If you disprove your belief in any way, revise it. State what idea it can replace according to your observation during the experiment and your conclusion.

Belief:
General prediction:
Specific prediction:
Experiment:
Observation of results:
Conclusion:
Revised belief:

Worksheet: Behavioral experiment

Rob, a 44-year-old IT graduate, owned an IT consulting firm where he invested much personal time, effort, and money. Over many years, his business grew from a small enterprise run out of his garage into a large company that made him a high six-figure salary and employed a growing staff. As the business grew and Rob hired new employees, he continued to oversee all staff duties. Even when there were ten of them, he continually micromanaged their work. This was exhausting for him and demoralizing for his staff, especially as Rob became increasingly short-tempered and demanding. Ever more hyper-critical and impatient, he never missed a chance to call someone out for even the slightest mistake.

He had a high staff turnover, and Rob began to worry about how this would affect the business. Initially, he blamed the staff for not caring about the company's long-term success as much as he did and for being half-hearted, entitled, and lazy. Finally, after receiving honest feedback from his human resources department, he conceded he might need to rethink his leadership strategy.

1. He started by testing two of the central beliefs behind his heavy-handed managerial style:

- His staff would not do as well if he fully delegated their tasks instead of checking in repeatedly on their work.
- He was not a devoted business owner unless he involved himself with details of his staff's work.

2. His general predictions were:

- If he fully delegated tasks to his staff and they didn't do as well, the business would suffer due to decreased sales and a drop in revenue. A decline in after-sales service would ruin the reliable reputation of the company that had taken years to build. Not knowing what the staff was doing daily would make him anxious and sleepless. His self-esteem would take a hit if his business suffered in revenue and reputation.
- If he did not continue to pour himself into his supervisory duties as a boss, his staff would start to lose respect for him. They would cut corners and do as little work as possible because he was setting a poor example as someone who did not work hard. If hard work

had brought him this far, hard work would see him through to the end.

3. Specifically, Rob's predictions were:

- His employees, Dean and Ray, would lose sight of what made the brand unique and waste resources on misplaced and ineffective advertising, attracting no new clients if he did not work with them closely all the time.
- Isla, Jerome, Audrey, and Steve would also slack off if he did not supervise their routine activities; they would chat too much over breaks, make fewer phone calls, send fewer emails, close fewer sales, and waste company time for personal use.
- Ollie, Maria, and Malcolm would deliver minimal client support and follow-up and lose clients by taking too long to respond to major problems.
- Rachel, Audrey, and Ollie were still new to the business and needed to be trained as the others were; the other staff had been with the business longer but might be more complacent than the newcomers.
- His clients would notice a decrease in attentiveness to detail and care in the

company's services, leading them to uptick the number of online complaints and contact Rob to complain. The company would lose valued clients to Rob's competitors.

4. Rob ran the following experiment:

- He randomly chose five employees with varying levels of experience and time at the company. He decided to refrain from asking them for updates on their daily tasks for three weeks.
- At the same time, he kept requesting daily updates from the other five employees.

5. During the three weeks, Rob observed the following:

- His overall anxiety levels were higher in the first week but not as much as he had envisioned.
- Rob had planned and did use the extra time afforded in not overseeing the routine tasks of five employees to visit potential clients, attend industry-related events, and work out more.
- After three weeks, Rob checked in on the work of the five employees he had not micromanaged and saw they had continued to perform their

daily functions independently and without missing a beat. He checked online reviews and saw no uptick in negative reviews, nor did he receive complaints from dissatisfied customers.

- He noticed a palpable difference in the atmosphere around the employees to whom he had entrusted self-management compared to those he had continued to micromanage. The former seemed happier and more relaxed around him than the latter.
- He felt more appreciative toward the employees who had managed independently and felt a deeper trust in them to get on with work without his constant involvement.

6. After observing the results of the experiment, Rob concluded:

- His helicopter management style had not positively influenced results but unnecessarily contributed to his stress and that of his employees. He saw how he could allocate the time he usually spent checking on his employees more productively to personal and business goals.
- He would only need to review his staff's overall activities monthly to stay connected to his team

and the business, but not drive himself (and his staff) crazy. His involvement in the daily nitty-gritty of his business was not crucial to the overall health of his company; instead, delegating was better for him, his staff, and the company overall.

7. He revised his beliefs to be:

- His staff would do as good a job if he fully delegated tasks without checking their work unnecessarily and repeatedly.
- He was more effective as a boss and leader when he did not control and oversee every detail of his staff's work.
- His staff was happier working for the company without his micromanaging behavior. This, in turn, would mean retaining good employees in whom he had invested resources and time in training.

MISTAKE-MAKING THERAPY

While the multi-dimensional definition of perfectionism defines the concept, the cognitive behavioral model for perfectionism describes how perfectionism manifests in thoughts and associated behavior.

According to the cognitive behavioral model for perfectionism, individuals base self-worth on performance. They develop rigid standards, cognitive biases, and performance-related behavior leading to the following three outcomes (Redden et al., 2022):

- Temporarily meeting standards.
- Failing to meet standards.
- Avoiding trying to meet standards.

Each outcome leads to self-critical and self-defeating behavior, even when meeting standards. When someone meets a perfect standard, they feel obliged to meet it again in the future. However, they will suspect the bar was too low, raise their expectations, fail to meet them, or avoid trying.

Exposure-based therapy for perfectionism, also known as exposure and response prevention or mistake-making therapy (MMT), is one way of breaking the ever-tightening downward spiral of perfectionism. Related to CBT but centered on intentional mistake-making, MMT aims to habituate patients to making mistakes. While CBT's primary goal is to test and disprove dysfunctional beliefs, MMT seeks to normalize and reduce the distress associated with the fear of failure. As hard as it is at first, the perfectionist intentionally lets things remain imperfect or makes intentional mistakes. As they see the consequences of imperfection are not as severe as they supposed or that they can handle them, it becomes easier to let imperfection in.

Imperfections, which must be deliberately included or allowed, should be small to start with, such as not making the bed every morning or letting a misspelled word go uncorrected. Gradually, increased exposure to the more distressing imperfections, such as inviting a friend to come when there are dirty dishes in the kitchen sink or when your home looks unkept. It may be hard to believe initially, but breaking free of typical ways of doing things and intentionally defying your perfection by being imperfect can be a fun and freeing experience.

Often, the mistakes we make are comforting to other people who feel more relaxed in the company of someone with flexible standards; those who judge us would do so anyway, and those who do not may feel relieved you, too, make mistakes. One of the most admirable traits in people, for me, is the ability not to take oneself too seriously—even to laugh at oneself with refreshing humor, unafraid to appear weak—and I try to remember to emulate the warm, approachable people in my life who make fools of themselves without self-reproach and shame.

If you feel like practicing MMT on yourself, Drs. Jacobs and Anthony (2019) have the following helpful pointers for beginners:

- Plan what you will be doing differently that invites imperfection and when, and anticipate outcomes. Repetition, predictability, and structure will initially make you feel more secure.
- "Let the imperfection be" until your discomfort decreases. If you try to fix it, you will defeat the exercise.
- Do not try to lessen your initial anxiety by trying to distract yourself or obtain exoneration or reassurance from others.
- Practice often because practice makes perfect— or in this case, practice makes imperfect, which is real progress!
- The more discomfort you can tolerate, the more imperfection you can live with daily, giving you a choice about where to place your efforts instead of feeling compelled to react perfectly, even when it doesn't matter.

Online MMT exposes perfectionists to clinically controlled mistake-making with immediate feedback to help them become used to making mistakes and less anxious about them. A recent study conducted to test the efficacy of a computerized, exposure-based treatment for perfectionism, to be completed at home every three days for two weeks for a total of five treatment sessions, showed participants exposed to mistake-making had lower overall perfectionism, concern over mistakes, personal standards, depressive symptoms, social anxiety symptoms, and error sensitivity than those not exposed to mistake-making (Redden et al., 2022).

If you suffer from perfectionism, you can defeat it by gradually loosening its hold on you by pushing yourself out of your comfort zone with MMT. The next chapter presents additional practical steps to stop your perfectionism from running you ragged. It is time to start to feel good enough as you are because you are good enough.

Admitting you are a perfectionist may be hard, as if you have made an even bigger mistake than any of the ones you were trying to avoid. You need to reach this point to be able to move forward. Perfectionism would still lie before you. Now, you can set out from here because you understand the fallacy that its name connotes and how destructive it can be. It is not about wiping out your perfectionism as if it never was or as something should never have existed: That would entail all-or-nothing thinking again.

Instead, you are building a better outlook, tailor-made for you, based on what you have learned from the lessons your perfectionism offers you.

7

PRACTICAL STEPS TO NON-PERFECTIONISM

W ho are you, really, underneath it all?

Follow the steps below without trying to force a quick fix or get it right immediately (more all-or-nothing thinking). Progress involves some meandering, shuffling, and back-stepping, like a dance. Without aiming for perfection but as part of your practice of non-perfection, set out on a journey of self-discovery as you work toward your goals.

From experience, I can say that although my goals have kept me going, the process of reaching them has been the best part of the journey. It has been full of surprises, twists, and turns, and I have learned so many things that are exciting about life, myself, and other people.

7 EFFECTIVE STEPS YOU CAN TAKE RIGHT AWAY

Track Your (Realistic) Goals

One way to confront problems with perfectionism is to set realistic goals. Identify the problems you want to address this week and consider how to challenge your perfectionism by doing things differently and *non-perfectly.*

Use the template below based on a table created by Dr. Jeremy Sutton (2021) to draft a weekly goal-tracker that will help manage your perfectionism.

Problem	General Goal	Specific Goal
E.g., Working long hours. Overdelivering.	Spend less time working and more time on non-achievement tasks.	Get to work only ten minutes early. Put work away at the end of the workday, no excuses. Go straight to the park for a walk after work. Do breathing and mindful exercises at the park. Make dinner as soon as I get home, complete only one important housework chore per day, and spend the rest of every evening doing something pleasurable.

Table 2: Weekly goal tracker to manage perfectionism

Take stock

Reflect on what perfectionism costs you in terms of:

- Time spent trying to attain perfection.
- Depleted mental capacity by ruminating or worrying.
- Opportunities passed up in pursuit of perfectionism.
- Intimacy and openness with those closest to you.

Shift your focus from perfection to your goal. Is your perfectionism contributing to it or detracting from it? Whatever you want, deep down, refuses to be obscured by perfectionist concerns. Using the cognitive-behavioral techniques discussed in the previous chapter, you can gain clarity with concrete evidence of what you do, why, and whether it works for you.

What are you working toward? Are you managing a project you hope will result in a job promotion? Do you want to be a teacher whose influence will continue positively affecting students' mindsets for the rest of their lives? Do you want to run a successful business? Spend time with your children before they grow up? Learn photography, flower arranging, or printmaking? Narrow your goals down to what is most important to you, but include both long-term, medium-term, and short-term goals and seemingly small and huge ones.

Gus, an eleven-year-old boy, showed a lot of promise in many subjects, from music to languages and history, and each of his teachers expected him to achieve high results. His coaches pushed him to achieve his best on the sports field. The minister at his church encouraged him to lead prayers and Bible readings, and he became involved in more than one charitable outreach organization. He relished the approval and praise he received from all quarters. But when anyone expressed disappointment in him, he was cut to the core. Several teachers and coaches seemed dissatisfied with his performance; some congregation members told him to speak up or slow down.

Eventually, he spread himself so thin across all his commitments that his grades plummeted. He missed homework, rehearsals, and practice and stopped caring enough to be excused. When his mother was mortified to discover him drinking alcohol with some of his friends, she ground him: But an interesting thing happened — for the first time since preschool, he caught up on sleep, spent time reading, drawing, and daydreaming, and bonded with his dog. The time-out turned out to be less of a punishment than a blessing. Gus realized he would survive if school, sports, church, and charities got by without him, and they did. He was still well-liked by many, especially those with whom he truly wanted to spend his time, doing well at what mattered most. Gus concentrated on his music, math, and computer science. He selected one sport, dropped the ones he did not care for, and learned to say no to church work and volunteering when he did not feel like it. Much to his mother's relief, it turned out drinking was not a preferred pastime of his after all.

Former clinical psychologist and author Alice Boyes states high achievers are bound to do some things imperfectly; to be productive and use time wisely, you will be "less perfect about some things, so you can concentrate on what's important" (Knight, 2019). There comes the point when you can overwork for little or no reward or even undo previous efforts. You pour all your attention into every detail and get lost in an all-consuming vortex of concentration, forgetting to step back and see the big picture.

The law of diminishing returns is an economic theory that predicts that when optimal capacity is reached, investing more in production will result in less rather than more efficient operation (Hayes, 2022). Once I have done enough work, in other words, doing more or overworking will reduce the rewarding results the work ultimately delivers. For instance, if I have worked out a settlement that my client is pleased with, continuing "working it" and asking for more from the other side may become counterproductive and even lead to cold feet or complications.

Psychologist Olivia Guy-Evans explains the Pareto Principle states that 20% effort leads to 80% returns. It was named after a 19th-century economist who discovered 80% of wealth and land in Italy and most countries were owned by 20% of people, in the same way 20% of the pea pods in his garden yielded 80% of the peas. Psychologist Joseph Juran later stated the Pareto Principle could be applied as a "universal principle," helping people to focus on the fewer main parts of a complex system rather than all its many trivial parts, spending a shorter time on essential activities rather than a long time on trivialities (Guy-Evans, 2022). The Pareto Principle is one of the biggest game changers for me in how I've come to see perfectionism — a surefire way to violate this time-tested concept routinely.

Set SMART goals

Goals give you something concrete to work toward but should not be unrealistic or grandiose. SMART is an acronym for (Petersen, 2022):

Specific: What exactly do you want to accomplish?

Measurable: Use the table of perfectionism in Chapter 5, the worksheet for the behavioral experiment in Chapter 6, the goal tracker above, and other methods you think of yourself to measure your progress.

Achievable: Start with easily attainable goals but challenge yourself with goals that are harder to reach but never unreasonable or unrealistic.

Realistic/Relevant: Goals should be practical and meaningful to you to be more likely to reach them. Not attaining them is okay, though. They are there to guide you rather than test you. As you establish your goals, remember some of them should not be achievement-based: They can include things such as spending time with people you care about, journaling, going to the beach or a natural area near you, watching a documentary or a movie, seeing your favorite band perform live, and so on.

Time-bound: Timelines or set periods will help you to see how long it takes to reach your goals and keep you motivated to complete the tasks. If you do not meet your deadline, reconsider whether your goal is realistic and relevant; if it is, give yourself more time to get there.

Make a checklist

Pursuing perfection is like wandering aimlessly on a journey without getting closer to your destination. Creating a checklist for each goal can help you map your journey with smaller checkpoints. You can cross them off and consider yourself done with them as you pass them. Try to keep the list short and in an easily accessible place so you do not accumulate many lists of no practical use. The checklist is not a way to accomplish your tasks as much as it is a way to measure your progress and remind yourself of your priorities.

Prioritize

Related to the checklist point above, prioritize the approximate 20% effort needed to realize 80% of your greater goal. Give yourself a break when it comes to the less critical tasks, thereby distributing your mental, physical, and emotional energy in a way that supports the bigger picture.

After my burnout and recovery with my sister's help, I realized I was putting too much time into my work, adding belts and suspenders that did not add value. Now I prioritize the steps that are going to help me deliver the big picture in a case or project, and I start once I have sight of the big picture; I stick with this without following superfluous logic or getting side-tracked, and I reserve energy and effort for what is going to move the needle on the main objective.

Seek Other Perspectives

Speaking to people worthy of your confidence, whom you trust, can act as a sounding board for your ideas. They don't even have to respond for you to hear yourself and gain perspective. As they are people you trust, you might as well tell them you are working on perfectionistic tendencies and need their help. You should understand you are not in this alone: we all need the help of others. When you were a baby, you could not fend for yourself and needed someone to feed and keep you safe. There were times when you felt as if you could not rely on anyone but yourself, and this feeling sharpened your inclination toward being perfect. Perfection might have meant self-sufficiency to you. But as humans, we are not self-sufficient: We have survived this far by relying on one another and working in groups.

Sarah is remarkably self-sufficient. Perfectionism has helped her achieve much within the multinational company where she works. But it has also been a constant source of anxiety and feelings of impostorism in connection with her performance. During large group meetings at work, she sometimes feels petrified and does not comment or offer input; she doubts the soundness of what she says and decides to say nothing. Before an important meeting where she wanted to provide input, she asked a trusted colleague, Scott, to give her objective feedback on her ideas. He obliged, and Sarah, consequently confident her comments were helpful and insightful, was the first to offer input after a short presentation by another colleague. As a result, she received a good response from management and got the ball rolling to initiate further dialogue on her views.

Limit social media

We have already seen how social media can exacerbate perfectionist tendencies. It should not be anyone's primary mode of communication. Below are some strategies to combat perfectionist tendencies in connection to social media (Lybsin, 2022):

- Be aware of the *unreality* of social media.
- View social media as a helpful tool for building social networks and friendships that should be further enhanced offline. Again, it only works as a primary mode of communication.

- Initiate conversations with young people to understand how social media affects them generally and individually.
- Understand perfection is inherently inhuman.
- Teach children, teenagers, and adults that authentic beauty resides in imperfection.
- Follow body-positive and other content that has nothing to do with physical appearance.
- Monitor the time you spend on social media. Take occasional complete breaks from it as a detox. If or when you return to it, you will hopefully see you didn't miss as much as you thought you would. People will grow used to your being intermittently unavailable or offline. You don't need to be permanently attached to your phone. If someone needs to get hold of you, they will find a way.
- Never ignore someone you are with as you check your phone. As a rule, if I must look at my phone while I am with someone, I explain why and what I am doing so they know I am not simply more interested in it than them.

5 TAILORED TIPS FOR EACH DIMENSION OF PERFECTIONISM

Self-oriented perfectionists (SOPs) don't attribute their stress to having standards that are impossible to meet but rather to failing to meet them. If you are an SOP:

Conduct a reality check on yourself

Objectively assess whether your goal is realistic or whether you have set yourself an unlikely or impossible goal.

Is there a *need* or feeling of deficit you have created a goal to fulfill?

Self-awareness, which requires asking yourself questions about the reasons behind your standards and beliefs, will help you disengage from unrealistic goals, become more flexible, and re-engage with goals that are more achievable and do not arise from a place of fear.

Socially prescribed perfectionists (SPPs), you will recall from Chapter 1, are overly concerned about others' criticism of them, fearing judgment and rejection. If you are an SPP:

Visualize your "worst-case scenario" and how to mitigate it

Play the worst-case scenario in your head to the end and beyond, to what might happen after the worst case. Visualize the ramifications and how you would cope.

You may realize the actual worst-case scenario and its aftermath is not as catastrophic an event as the anxious you may want to believe. For example, Barry constantly worries about losing his job due to failing to deliver the best sales results for his team. He makes a subconscious, "short-circuit" connection between being out of work and homeless. But suppose Barry plays it all out in his head calmly and logically. He would realize that should he lose his job, the company would be obliged to pay a six-month severance package per his contract, and he might even be able to negotiate a bit more; after working for them, his resume is more impressive so he is likely to land an even better job by the time his severance runs out; he has savings; and his spouse also works, so they will not be destitute while he finds new work.

By doing this exercise, you may also realize the worst-case scenario for your fear is not the most likely outcome.

Focus on mastery, not performance

Performance-focused goals are concerned with measuring oneself against others. You might try to outperform others or not perform worse than them. Mastery-focused goals, in contrast, are focused on self-improvement and learning. You measure your progress against your previous performance. When you are competing against yourself, you will find the achievements of others do not threaten you as they would if you were competing against them. You will be less inclined to see another person's strengths as somehow contributing to your weakness or wish to put people down to feel better.

When you don't have the pressure of being evaluated by others, you feel safer experimenting, taking risks, deviating where necessary, learning, and growing.

Remember the dimensions of perfectionism can overlap. You need not fit into a neatly labeled box, and one size only fits some, but the tips and tools offered here will work for you if you use them regularly and make them your own.

Other-oriented perfectionists (OOPs) make exacting and inflexibly high demands for perfection on others. If you are an OOP:

Train your empathy and patience

When you are about to get an automatic reaction to someone's mistake, catch yourself before lashing out with anger or reproach. Make a point of shifting your focus from the perceived fault to what that person has done well, either then or in the past.

Negativity bias in humans means we consider negative aspects of a person or situation more important and worthy of attention than positive ones (Frothingham, 2019). This bias was genetically inherited from ancient ancestors whose survival depended on noticing danger and immediately escaping it. As important as the positive elements of life were, such as finding food or making social alliances, people had to constantly remain vigilant and prepared to interrupt any other activity with the fight, flight, freeze, or fawn response discussed in Chapter 1. To be always alert to negatives is, by implication, an archaic approach to life.

It is a sign of maturity and generosity to reinforce people positively when you appreciate what they say or do.

Pay grace forward

Instead, pay grace forward. Reflect on times when you messed up and someone gracefully let you off the hook and did not rub it in; they might have helped you get out of trouble. It felt good, and you were grateful. Remember to pay that forward in your daily encounters with others and when you find someone makes a mistake.

If you can admit and forgive your mistakes, it will be easier to pardon others' mistakes too. It takes a certain amount of humility to be gracious; acknowledging you are not perfect, seeing your faults without trying to hide them, and persevering regardless of shortcomings will keep you humble but strong. When you realize how much forgiveness you can give, you become more forgiving of others. Gratitude is directly related to grace and can touch and enrich every aspect of life.

This leads us to the last chapter about mindfulness, or developing the habit of being nonjudgmental about events, others, and yourself.

8

THE MINDFULNESS TOOLKIT

Mindfulness and perfectionism are incompatible and cannot co-exist. Practicing mindfulness is an excellent way of defeating perfectionistic concerns.

Professor Jon Kabat-Zinn, who brought mindfulness to the fore in improving mental wellness and quality of life and founded the Mindfulness-Based Stress Reduction Program, defines mindfulness as "the awareness that arises from paying attention, on purpose, in the present moment, and non-judgmentally" (Masterclass, 2021). Clinics implemented his remarkably effective program to help outpatients with chronic pain and other medical conditions who weren't responding to conventional therapy to change their mental and physical relationship to their experiences.

Perfectionists place people's worth not in who they are but in their actions. Simply being is regarded as an inadequate reason for acceptance in society. In her Mindfulness Workbook for Perfectionism (2022), Dr. Elaine Thomas emphasizes perfectionists can practice mindfulness and reap its benefits but practicing how to be rather than do. She highlights that, contrary to widespread belief, mindfulness is scientifically sound and evidence-based, with mindfulness-based cognitive therapy studies proving its efficacy in alleviating perfectionist problems, such as rumination, stress, and other mental health issues.

Research also shows mindfulness helps with perceived stress and social anxiety, both outcomes of perfectionistic tendencies (Wang et al., 2022).

6 MINDFULNESS PRACTICES TO ENRICH YOUR LIFE

As a significant part of my recovery from perfectionism, I learned mindfulness; it still serves me well and has become an indispensable part of my daily routine. I would be remiss not to share some mindfulness tools I have learned along the way, and I urge you to implement them in your life and make consistent use of them.

Non-Judgment

This one is hard for perfectionists, but you should strive to practice non-judgment towards yourself and others.

Drs. Flett, Hewitt, Nepon, and Besser's Perfectionism Cognition Theory (Stoeber, 2018) describes the thoughts and inner criticisms perfectionists engage in. They go something like this:

- I need to do better.
- I should never make mistakes.
- I should be doing more.
- I must work hard all the time.
- I wonder what others think of me and my work.
- I am afraid I won't do well.
- I would be a loser if I did not set high standards for myself.
- I'm not as good as other people.

Which ones are familiar to you and part of your inner critic? If I finished my work in less time than I had budgeted for it, instead of using that spare time on other things, I would wonder if I had done as much as I ought to and return to the work to review it and add to it. If anyone suggested changes to my work, I should have been more thorough than they had in looking over it. "Even when I work overtime," I thought, "I can't get it right." I wanted to be self-sufficient and hated relying on anyone else for input or advice.

Next time judgmental thoughts like these surface, use the STOP technique (Thomas, 2022):

1. Stop

Pause. In that space between stimulus (thought) and response (stress, worry, or shame), we can pause and choose how to react.

2. Take a conscious breath

Breathe deeply, hold your breath, and slowly exhale. Do this at least 4 to 5 times. Concentrate on your breathing instead of your thoughts. Conscious breathing is a beneficial activity you can perform about anywhere. It fools the body into believing all is well by soothing our vagus nerve, which is responsible for our parasympathetic nervous system. When we are relaxed, we breathe slowly and deeply. Our breathing becomes shallow and irregular when our fight, flight, freeze, or fawn response gets triggered. But if we breathe slowly and deeply anyway, even under stress, our body and mind respond as if the danger has passed.

3. Observe what is going on in your body and mind

Acknowledge how your thoughts have made you feel, physically and emotionally.

Your body and mind are not separate entities; when the mind is well, the body benefits, and vice versa. If any physical activity helps you feel as if you are more present in your body than usual or enables you to get out of your head, make time for that exercise.

For me, it is cross-training. Cycling, weightlifting, yoga, hiking, and gardening help me stay fit and provide a break from my work environment. I spend a lot of time in my head and must try to balance cerebral and visceral activities. The natural landscape welcomes me with open arms when I walk or hike. When I garden, I love to dig deep into the soil and smell the rich, loamy soil. Being in nature is a beautiful way to bring body and mind together. My mind becomes clearer, and my body feels stronger.

4. Proceed with what you were doing

The unwelcome perfectionist thought interrupted your flow. Pick up from where you left off.

You can say to yourself, "This may be my perfectionist side talking, and it does not represent the whole of me."

You can actively distance yourself from perfectionist thoughts by reframing them with something like this:

> *I am having the thought that I need to do better.*
> *The thought has occurred to me that I should never make mistakes.*
> *The thought has crossed my mind that I should be doing more.*

Instead of blaming yourself for feeling imperfect, you pin the responsibility on the thought, discard it as your negative perfectionism talking, and move on.

Self-Compassion

Mindfulness works together with self-compassion, which may not come naturally to everyone, but it is a skill that can be learned. Being mindful of your perfectionism and the psychological pain it causes can help you know and experience it for what it is and accept yourself as you are. This will show you can be kind and comfort yourself, lifting the burden you or your upbringing placed upon your shoulders. You can be your own best friend and good to yourself, whether you think you deserve it or not.

Steps to express your self-acceptance and compassion:

- **Become more aware of your body**

Sometimes our psychological stress is physically palpable to us, but we ignore it, conditioned to it as we have become.

Pay attention to how your body feels at any given moment. Think about the position of your body, your posture and stance, whether your muscles are tight in places, how your head and neck are connected, your shoulders to your arms, your legs to your feet, and so on. Purposefully play with the tension in your limbs, relax your mouth and jaw, close your eyes, and roll your shoulder blades.

Place your feet firmly on the floor and focus on the feeling of the connection between your soles and what is beneath them. Standing barefoot on the earth so you feel connected with it is wonderfully comforting. You are a natural being, just like the earth you stand on. Sense your placement in your surroundings and your physical relationship to the things around you.

- **Use your five senses to keep you in the present reality of your body**

Treat your body well by eating when you are hungry and eating something delicious and nutritious.

Take a walk and notice how your legs swing and your body sways. Link the rhythm of your walking to your breathing. Break your rhythm with a skip or jump.

- **Try to release your feelings through the movements of your body**

Lie down and rest. Massage your neck, feet, or hands. You are your own caregiver. Or get a professional scalp or body massage (or both) and let yourself feel all the sensations that connect you to your skin and sense of touch. Anything you can do to improve your physical comfort, pleasure, and health will put stress, anxiety, and worry in perspective for that moment in time. The more you practice these activities, the more of a habit you will form of disconnecting from your perfectionism and connecting with your body.

- **Write to yourself**

If there is an event from the past you find yourself ruminating about, such as when someone hurt or offended you or you did something you regret, write a letter to yourself. Describe the situation objectively and as you would to someone who wasn't there. But please remove any trace of blame or shame. Do not include sentences about what you should have done or said or second-guess the reasons behind what happened.

As you write this letter, you will begin to see the incident from the outside, as if you were reading part of someone else's letter to you. Instead of judging yourself, the letter should help you empathize with your situation and how you handled it and let you release it.

- **Encourage yourself**

If your good friend found herself in a tricky situation, you would not judge them but be supportive and encouraging, especially if they were being hard on themselves or expected too much. You would realize you would merely add to their distress by criticizing them or acting as if you had all the answers. If they told you, "I am an idiot! I always get it wrong," you probably would disagree with them and tell them how to get it right next time.

When you find yourself in a comparable situation, direct the same sort of compassionate responses for a good friend toward yourself.

Instead of negative self-talk, say positive, reinforcing things to yourself. Put things into perspective, and do not generalize.

Often, when a friend or someone else makes a mistake, we believe their problem is one they will overcome. We can apply this perspective to our own errors and challenges by understanding they seem worse to us than they are. It has happened so often—I feel overwhelmed by a problem, only to forget it once it has passed. Remember those times and use them as reminders to put the current problem in its proper perspective.

Radical Acceptance

Radical acceptance means accepting situations beyond your control without judgment, thereby reducing the suffering they cause you; instead of becoming emotionally involved with the suffering, you welcome reality for what it is. It differentiates between pain and suffering: Pain is the reality, but suffering is the individual's response to the pain. If you do not accept the pain, you will prolong your suffering. The idea has Buddhist origins and radical acceptance is based on the model presented by psychologist Carl Rogers that acceptance is the first step toward change (Cuncic, 2021).

Radical acceptance is not about giving up on a goal. It involves relinquishing efforts to control that which we cannot control. It is essential to be able to tell the difference. If we keep trying to control something beyond us, we cannot move on and consider our other options. As a lawyer, I meet many people who resist the inevitable, battling to come to terms with it and continuing to run against an immovable obstacle long after they should have found another way. I advise people not to become fixated on an imagined outcome but to remain open to other ideas. There is usually more than one solution to any problem. People who wish for what might have been become stuck, consumed by resentment, and worn out with frustration.

We often do not have absolute clarity about the outcomes of important decisions in our lives, no matter how much we may weigh the pros and cons ahead of the decision. Ultimately, you must make a choice, think about the life you will live after making that choice, and then move forward with your decision. A lot about life is full of uncertainty. We should get comfortable with the discomfort that comes with knowing that and embrace, or radically accept, that truth. There is beauty and bewilderment in the unknown, so learn to let go of the impulse to try to control all outcomes. You won't be able to, for better or worse, and that's part of the magic of life!

Gratitude

Dr. Erica Hamilton reminds us that "The mind can sometimes get conditioned to look for flaws. Gratitude really shifts what our search function is, looking for what we have already achieved, or already accomplished" (2023).

To practice gratitude:

- **Meditate**

You don't have to be a seasoned meditator to meditate on what you are grateful for. Just take some quiet time for yourself when you can center your thoughts around what you appreciate in your life, whether big or small, lasting, or fleeting, from others or thanks to you. You can be thankful to yourself for all kinds of things, including being thankful.

There are countless free or paid subscription resources online or in-person to learn how to meditate. There are many diverse types of meditation practice. However, the overarching goal should be to quiet the mind's thoughts, sit still in peace and feel a sense of calmness and gratitude.

- **Put your gratitude into words**

Start and end every day with a sincere Thank You. For those who believe in God, prayer works well; for those who do not, you may be grateful to a greater life force, universal intelligence, or the earth. Keeping a gratitude journal shows you how much to be thankful for. I compile a list every day before going to sleep. Sometimes I switch my bedside lamp on several times because I think of more items I want to add. I often find myself smiling as I lie down. "Thank you for the quietness and calm of this moment; Thank you for giving me a purpose today; Thank you for a refreshing glass of water; Thank you for the roof over my head," and so on. The more you practice gratitude, the longer your list will become.

- **Tell others what you appreciate about them**

Now and then, please make a point of telling someone you appreciate something about them. People love to be thanked, and thanking people is just as pleasurable. Again, smiles usually follow.

- **Write a letter of thanks**

A person will be truly touched if you take the time to thank them in writing for what they have done for you. You can send a voice note or text, but a lovely card or letter is extra special. Even though I am far from being a hoarder, I cannot throw away Thank You cards. They remind me of my goodness as well as the goodness of others.

Celebration

Celebrating successes, no matter how small, is vital to overcoming Impostor Syndrome and related feelings of low self-esteem and inadequacy.

Focusing on how successes make you feel is important to remind you your thoughts matter as much as what you did. External validation and reward do not motivate as much as an internal sense of satisfaction and accomplishment. So even if no one else understands why what you did is worth celebrating, if you feel delighted or proud about it, celebrate!

Celebration can be as simple as leaping into the air with a shout or as complicated as eating sushi under a starry sky with champagne and three of your best friends — but whatever you do, enjoy the moment.

Process not Product

Concentrate on the process, not the product. You can miss opportunities when you are single-minded and future focused. After identifying the goals that matter most to you, live in the moment to enjoy reaching them rather than thinking only of the result. Learning as one goes along makes the journey at least as important as the destination. Remember progress is rarely linear but full of twists, turns, lessons, and deviations. Yet progress is what we are after, not unattainable perfection.

In retrospect, I usually loved the times when I was surprised when unpredictable things happened, and I was able to adjust accordingly. Such as, when I caught the wrong bus during a vacation in Portugal and went somewhere I never planned to go, to a colorful and bohemian side of town I never knew existed; I found a stationery shop unlike any I had ever seen and, stationery is one of my weaknesses. I spent over an hour there. These times of discovery and exploration can make the most inspiring times of our lives; may we never grow tired or disinterested when there is always so much to discover around us!

My friend, the artist Iris, teaches her students that painting is about process rather than product. "You end up with a painting," she says, "But it is just what is left after art making, which is the first part of the process. People think the painting itself—the thing—can be valued and worth investing in. But no painting, not even the most famous, is valuable without the second part of the process, where the viewer comes in. By viewer, I do not mean a critic or a collector, but a random person like you or me who looks at the painting. If they actively look at the painting, engage with it, and let it stir something in them, they are the second part of the painting process. They complete the process by bringing something of themselves to the painting: They respond, think, and feel." She nods and dabs at her canvas. "Good artists don't make products; they create a process."

When I asked her about perfectionism and art, she smiled, "Don't even go there!"

I continued watching her paint, in silence, for a while. She sweeps red color over pink, with a smear of blue on the edge, then stops to look at me, wiping her fingers on an old turpentine-soaked rag. "Perfectionism smothers life, and life is what art is all about."

Perfectionists may be more inclined than most to consider their worth as product-related or performance-based because products or results seem easier to measure than processes. But it's precisely in the mess that is the process where we should find our inspiration, the beauty in life, and our "good enough."

CONCLUSION

Is your perfectionism critical to your identity or critical *of* it?

Sorting out perfectionism and the problems it brings is not an overnight goal. Still, step by step, focusing on the central issues that affect your quality of life, you will slowly cultivate a beautifully personal non-perfectionism.

This book has empowered you to start dealing with your perfectionistic tendencies as a problematic part of your life rather than something that might benefit you. We have defined what perfectionism is and established it is not beneficial. We have discussed the causes and symptoms of perfectionism. You have looked at yourself and your behavior and beliefs to decide whether you have perfectionistic habits. Probably realizing you do, you have discovered useful advice and techniques to return to the path that leads to your primary goals, and to enjoy the process of getting there.

This book should not replace professional care if you feel you need it. There are many options for professional therapy, and you will find one that is right for you. Search online, inquire about reputable establishments, and obtain recommendations and references. Remember you will need the help of others at some stages of your life. It is wise to ask someone you trust to support you or assist you in finding support if your perfectionism is ruining your mental health.

Returning to the topic of my love of music — as I watched the pianist Hélène Grimaud play the Steinway Grand at a concert, it occurred to me many great pianists have played the classical piece she was playing before her. If the goal were simply to play the music, it would have been achieved many times. Some might argue another pianist can play the same piece at a higher level. But I was not there to see previous renditions. For me, this is what I enjoyed and what my senses heard, and I was deeply moved by it.

To all appearances, she is a perfect musician. But there is an element of vulnerability and honesty to her that goes beyond perfection. Grimaud is left-handed (which once upon a time would have been considered by her teachers to be a trait that needed correction), and she has synesthesia, associating colors with keys (Piano Street, 2013). One can sense there are colors in her mind's eye as she plays.

The performance felt more like an experience than a show; it pulled me in, inviting me to participate. At no time did I feel the need to judge what I was hearing. I was simply swept along, taking part in the life of the music from its inception in the composer's mind to its manifestation there and now.

The music and what we see and feel as the performer plays make it a singular, never-to-be-repeated moment in time. Each of us is on a journey; although we share it, it is different for each of us. There are all kinds of memories and emotions the music stirred in me, too layered and numerous to decipher.

When I was learning to play the piano, my classmates and I felt our music teachers expected too much of us and wanted us to play perfectly. Some of those teachers may have been other-oriented perfectionists. Still, what we needed to remember was that we were developing skills and the more we practiced, the better we would be. It was a skill worth acquiring even if we played "badly" for a long time, because it would enrich us in many ways.

We could see how discipline and determination paid off and how ongoing practice was necessary to acquire a skill. Rather than regard our lessons as a way of pointing out our lack of knowledge and inability, we needed to see them as a way of increasing our musical experience. Perfectionism comes from a place of lack and a deficit mindset. Non-perfectionists know mistakes and struggles lead to greater gains and nurture a growth mindset. Instead of saying, "I am bad at piano and hate going to lessons," I had to say to myself, "I will improve, and I'm starting to enjoy the lessons." I did. Later, I applied the same thinking to my situation at work, where I had allowed debilitating perfectionism to creep in. "I can't do this anymore, and I dread work," became, "I will find another way of doing this, and work will become rewarding again."

To be excellent at something you care about is liberating: You reach a place of ease or a sweet spot where thought and effort seem replaced by intuition and feeling. It happens in all spheres, from dancing to rock climbing, when skills become subconscious. But there is always more to learn, and sometimes we must go back to the basics and concentrate hard again after we make a mistake, encounter self-doubt, or experience anxiety due to a significant life change.

No one else can be you more perfectly than you; you are imperfect by design. You know what I mean when I say, "perfect imperfection." Every individual life on earth has this quality. Preconceived notions and cognitive biases can smother it, or it can be recognized and protected. You can find that quality in yourself and nourish it, understanding it will have flaws.

You can do this with the insights, tools, and disciplines you have learned after reading this book. Once you use the tools provided, you will start to see a change in yourself, and others will too. Less anxiety, stress, worry, and rumination will make you more approachable. You will notice how much more relaxed and friendly people seem when they are around you. Instead of the reproach and rejection for being imperfect, you will receive leniency and acceptance, most significantly, from yourself. You will start to like yourself more, even if you aren't always right—perhaps because you aren't. Your newfound authenticity will be endearing and courageous. You will recover your strength and energy because you will no longer be battling yourself and others over the unattainable.

That is why I wrote this book: You are too unique and special to hide your light. As another great musician, Leonard Cohen, sang in his iconic anthem released over thirty years ago, "Ring the bell which still can ring.

Forget your perfect offering. There is a crack, a crack in everything. That's how the light gets in" (2020).

If you enjoyed and learned from this book, that was the goal of *my* process. Please leave a review on Amazon for others who might benefit from reading it.

Now, all that is left to do is to practice your non-perfection, in all its glory. Enjoy the adventure!

REFERENCES

Benson, E. (2003, November). *The many faces of perfectionism*. American Psychological Association. https://www.apa.org/monitor/nov03/manyfaces

Burcaş, S., & Creţu, R. Z. (2021). Perfectionism and neuroticism: Evidence for a common genetic and environmental etiology. *Journal of Personality, 89*(4). https://doi.org/10.1111/jopy.12617

Byrne, S. (2023, February 4). *Karen Carpenter had a "quest for perfection" in her music that "carried over in her life," says biographer.* Yahoo Entertainment. https://www.yahoo.com/entertainment/karen-carpenter-death-anniversary-biographer-randy-schmidt-165727243.html?guccounter=1

Cherry, K. (2022, October 19). *The big five personality traits*. Verywell Mind. https://www.verywellmind.com/the-big-five-personality-dimensions-2795422

Clance, P. R. (1985). *The Impostor Phenomenon*. Peachtree Pub Limited.

Cohen, L. (2020). Leonard Cohen: Anthem (live in London) [Video]. YouTube. https://www.youtube.com/watch?v=c8-BT6y_wYg

Cokley, K., Stone, S., Krueger, N., Bailey, M., Garba, R., & Hurst, A. (2018). Self-esteem as a mediator of the link between perfectionism and the impostor phenomenon. *Personality and Individual Differences, 135*, 292–297. https://doi.org/10.1016/j.paid.2018.07.032

Cuncic, A. (2021, May 26). *What is radical acceptance?* Verywell Mind. https://www.verywellmind.com/what-is-radical-acceptance-5120614

Curran, T., & Hill, A. P. (2019). Perfectionism is increasing over time: A meta-analysis of birth cohort differences from 1989 to 2016. *Psychological Bulletin, 145*(4), 410–429. https://doi.org/10.1037/bul0000138

Drinks, T. (n.d.). *ADHD and perfectionism*. Understood. https://www.understood.org/en/articles/adhd-and-perfectionism

Dryden, J. (2018, July 18). *Perfectionism in young children may indicate OCD risk*. Washington University School of Medicine in St. Louis. https://medicine.wustl.edu/news/perfectionism-in-young-children-may-indicate-ocd-risk/

Fitzgerald, F. S. (1925). The Great Gatsby. Charles Scribner's Sons.

Frothingham, S. (2019, December 17). *Do you have a negativity bias?* Healthline. https://www.healthline.com/health/negativity-bias#overview

Garnham, C. (2022, May 13). *The Gen Z mental health wave - what is causing the surge?* HealthMatch. https://healthmatch.io/blog/the-gen-z-mental-health-wave-what-is-causing-the-surge

Goop. (n.d.). *Why perfectionism is on the rise and how to overcome it*. Goop. https://goop.com/wellness/mindfulness/why-perfectionism-is-on-the-rise-and-how-to-overcome-it/

Guy-Evans, O. (2022, November 3). *Pareto Principle (the 80-20 rule): Examples & more*. Simply Psychology. https://simplypsychology.org/pareto-principle.html

Hamachek, D. E. (1978). Psychodynamics of normal and neurotic perfectionism. *Psychology: A Journal of Human Behavior, 15*(1), 27–33. https://psycnet.apa.org/record/1979-08598-001

Hargreaves, R. (1994). *Mr. Perfect*. World International, Egmont Books Ltd. https://archive.org/details/mrperfect0000harg_g6r7/page/n40/mode/1up?view=theater

Harvard Medical School. (2019). *4 ways to boost your self-compassion*. Harvard Health Publishing. https://www.health.harvard.edu/mental-health/4-ways-to-boost-your-self-compassion

Hawgood, A. (2022, March 5). *What is "bigorexia"?* The New York Times. https://www.nytimes.com/2022/03/05/style/teen-bodybuilding-bigorexia-tiktok.html

Hayes, A. (2022, April 4). *Law of diminishing marginal returns*. Investopedia. https://www.investopedia.com/terms/l/lawofdiminishingmarginalreturn.asp

Hellmann, E. (2016). *Keeping up appearances: perfectionism and perfectionistic self-presentation on social media*. [Honor Scholar thesis, DePauw University]. https://scholarship.depauw.edu/studentresearch/50/

Herman, W. E. (2011). *Identity formation*. Encyclopedia of Child Behavior and Development. https://doi.org/10.1007/978-0-387-79061-9_1443

Hewitt, P. L. (2020). Perfecting, belonging, and repairing: A dynamic-relational approach to perfectionism. *Canadian Psychology/Psychologie Canadienne, 61*(2), 101–110. https://doi.org/10.1037/cap0000209

Hewitt, P. L., Flett, G. L., Sherry, S. B., Habke, M., Parkin, M., Lam, R. W., McMurtry, B., Ediger, E., Fairlie, P., & Stein, M. B. (2003). The interpersonal expression of perfection: Perfectionistic self-presentation and psychological distress. *Journal of Personality and Social Psychology, 84*(6), 1303–1325. https://doi.org/10.1037/0022-3514.84.6.1303

Hofmann, S. G. (2007). Cognitive factors that maintain social anxiety disorder: A comprehensive model and its treatment implications. *Cognitive Behaviour Therapy, 36*(4), 193–209. https://doi.org/10.1080/16506070701421313

Holland, G., & Marika Tiggemann. (2016, June). *A systematic review of the impact of the use of social networking sites on body image and disordered eating outcomes*. ResearchGate. https://www.researchgate.net/publication/298794212_A_systematic_review_of_the_impact_of_the_use_of_social_networking_sites_on_body_image_and_disordered_eating_outcomes

International OCD Foundation. (2023). *What is OCD?* International OCD Foundation. https://iocdf.org/about-OCD/

Jacobs, A. M., & Anthony, M. M. (2019). *Strategies for coping with the need to be perfect*. Beyond OCD. https://beyondocd.org/expert-perspectives/articles/the-search-for-imperfection-strategies-for-coping-with-the-need-to-be-perfe

Knight, R. (2019, April 29). *How to manage your perfectionism*. Harvard Business Review. https://hbr.org/2019/04/how-to-manage-your-perfectionism

Krogh, S. C., & Madsen, O. J. (2023). Dissecting the achievement generation: How different groups of early adolescents experience and navigate contemporary achievement demands. *Journal of Youth Studies*, *26*(2), 1–17. https://doi.org/10.1080/13676261.2022.2162812

Laurence, E. (2019, January 16). *The mindfulness techniques every perfectionist needs in their back pocket*. Well and Good. https://www.wellandgood.com/how-to-overcome-perfectionism/

Lybsin, L. (2022, October 28). *Raising good humans (S2 Ep 88): Mythbusting perfectionism with Professor Thomas Curran*. [Podcast]. Aliza.libsyn. https://aliza.libsyn.com/s2-ep-88-mythbusting-perfectionsm-with-professor-thomas-curran

Madsen, O. J. (2021). *Deconstructing Scandinavia's "achievement generation": A youth mental health crisis?* Palgrave Macmillan.

Masterclass. (2021, June 7). *Guide to Jon Kabat-Zinn: 14 Books by Jon Kabat-Zinn*. Masterclass. https://www.masterclass.com/articles/jon-kabat-zinn-book-guide

Merriam-Webster. (2019). *Definition of perfectionism*. Merriam-Webster. https://www.merriam-webster.com/dictionary/perfectionism

Merriam-Webster. (2022). *Definition of keep up with the Joneses*. Merriam-Webster. https://www.merriam-webster.com/dictionary/keep%20up%20with%20the%20Joneses

Merriam-Webster. (2023a). *Definition of perfection*. Merriam-Webster. https://www.merriam-webster.com/dictionary/perfection

Merriam-Webster. (2023b). Definition of perseverate. Merriam-Webster. https://www.merriam-webster.com/dictionary/perseverate

NHS. (2021, February 10). *Overview: Cognitive behavioural therapy (CBT)*. NHS UK. https://www.nhs.uk/mental-health/talking-therapies-medicine-treatments/talking-therapies-and-counselling/cognitive-behavioural-therapy-cbt/overview/

Niles, B. (Director). (2007, November). *Note by note: The making of Steinway L1037* [Film]. Argot Pictures.

O'Connor, B. (2022, October 14). *Why Gen Z are right to be worried about money*. BBC. https://www.bbc.com/worklife/article/20221013-why-gen-z-are-right-to-be-worried-about-money

Oakes, K. (2019, March 11). *The complicated truth about social media and body image*. BBC. https://www.bbc.com/future/article/20190311-how-social-media-affects-body-image

Page, O. (2022, February 28). *Imposter syndrome: 10 Best psychology books to overcome self-doubt*. Positive Psychology. https://positivepsychology.com/imposter-syndrome-books/

Pannhausen, S., Klug, K., & Rohrmann, S. (2020). Never good enough: The relation between the impostor phenomenon and multidimensional perfectionism. *Current Psychology, 41*. https://doi.org/10.1007/s12144-020-00613-7

Petersen, T. J. (2022, December 12). *How to overcome perfectionism: 12 Tips for success*. Choosing Therapy. https://www.choosingtherapy.com/how-to-overcome-perfectionism/

Petersson, S., Johnsson, P., & Perseius, K.I. (2017). A Sisyphean task: experiences of perfectionism in patients with eating disorders. *Journal of Eating Disorders, 5*(1). https://doi.org/10.1186/s40337-017-0136-4

Petre, A. (2019, October 30). *6 Common types of eating disorders (and their symptoms)*. Healthline. https://www.healthline.com/nutrition/common-eating-disorders

Piano Street. (2013, May 31). *Synesthesia: Do you have it? Can one develop it?* Piano Street. https://www.pianostreet.com/smf/index.php?topic=51279.0

Ramsay, J. R. (2019). *Adult ADHD and perfectionistic thoughts*. Apsard. http://apsard.org/wp-content/uploads/2019/10/Adult-ADHD-and-Perfectionistic-Thoughts.pdf

Redden, S. A., Patel, T. A., & Cougle, J. R. (2022). Computerized treatment of perfectionism through mistake making: A preliminary study. *Journal of Behavior Therapy and Experimental Psychiatry, 77*, 101771. https://doi.org/10.1016/j.jbtep.2022.101771

Reed, L. (1972). *Perfect Day* [Studio Album]. David Bowie & Mick Ronson. YouTube. https://youtu.be/QYEC4TZsy-Y

Research Gate. (2023, February 22). Perfectionism PDF. Research Gate. https://www.researchgate.net/publication/303370720_Perfectionism

Rnic, K., Hewitt, P. L., Chen, C., Jopling, E., Lemoult, J., & Flett, G. L.

(2021). Examining the link between multidimensional perfectionism and depression: A longitudinal study of the intervening effects of social disconnection. *Journal of Social and Clinical Psychology*, *40*(4), 277–303. https://doi.org/10.1521/jscp.2021.40.4.277

Rogers-de Jong, M. (n.d.). *Perfectionism & procrastination*. Navigation Psychology. https://www.navigationpsychology.com/blog/perfectionism-procrastination

Rozental, A. (2020). Beyond perfect? A case illustration of working with perfectionism using cognitive behavior therapy. *Journal of Clinical Psychology*, *76*(11), 2041–2054. https://doi.org/10.1002/jclp.23039

Ryan-Mosley, T. (2021, April 2). *Beauty filters are changing the way young girls see themselves*. MIT Technology Review. https://www.technologyreview.com/2021/04/02/1021635/beauty-filters-young-girls-augmented-reality-social-media/

Sandberg, S. (2013). *Lean in: Women, work, and the will to lead*. Knopf.

Shafran, R., Egan, S., & Wade, T. (2010). *Overcoming perfectionism*. Robinson.

Sherry, S. B., Hewitt, P. L., Flett, G. L., Lee-Baggley, D. L., & Hall, P. A. (2007). Trait perfectionism and perfectionistic self-presentation in personality pathology. *Personality and Individual Differences*, *42*(3), 477–490. https://doi.org/10.1016/j.paid.2006.07.026

Simmons, R. (2016, August 19). *How social media is a toxic mirror*. Time. https://time.com/4459153/social-media-body-image/

Stoeber, J. (2018). *The psychology of perfectionism: Theory, research, applications*. Routledge.

Stoeber, J., & Childs, J. H. (2011). *Perfectionism*. Encyclopedia of Adolescence.. https://doi.org/10.1007/978-1-4419-1695-2_279

Sutton, J. (2021, November 25). *How to overcome perfectionism: 15 Worksheets & resources*. Positive Psychology. https://positivepsychology.com/how-to-overcome-perfectionism/

The Learning Network. (2022, March 31). *What students are saying about how social media affects their body image*. The New York Times.

https://www.nytimes.com/2022/03/31/learning/what-students-are-saying-about-how-social-media-affects-their-body-image.html

Thomas, E. A. (2022). *Mindfulness workbook for perfectionism: Effective strategies to overcome your inner critic and find balance.* Rockridge Press.

Titus Lucretius Carus. (1743). *Of the nature of things, in six books.* Daniel Browne.

University of British Columbia. (2016, February 4). *February lab of the month: Dr. Paul Hewitt's pursuit of understanding perfectionism.* UBC Department of Psychology. https://psych.ubc.ca/news/lab-of-the-month-dr-paul-hewitts-pursuit-of-understanding-perfectionism/

Wang, Y., Chen, J., Zhang, X., Lin, X., Sun, Y., Wang, N., Wang, J., & Luo, F. (2022). The relationship between perfectionism and social anxiety: A moderated mediation model. *International Journal of Environmental Research and Public Health, 19*(19), 12934. https://doi.org/10.3390/ijerph191912934

Woodfin, V., Binder, P.-E., & Molde, H. (2020). The psychometric properties of the frost multidimensional perfectionism scale. *Frontiers in Psychology, 11.* https://doi.org/10.3389/fpsyg.2020.01860

Xie, Y., Kong, Y., & Yang, J. (2019). Perfectionism, worry, rumination, and distress: A meta-analysis of the evidence for the perfectionism cognition theory. *Personality and Individual Differences, 139*(1), 301–312. Research Gate. https://doi.org/10.1016/j.paid.2018.11.028

Yad Vashem. (2023). Francis Foley | www.yadvashem.org. Foley.html. https://www.yadvashem.org/righteous/stories/foley.html

www.ingramcontent.com/pod-product-compliance
Lightning Source LLC
Chambersburg PA
CBHW020251130626
46549CB00005B/2174